Profiles in Achievement

Profiles in Achievement

Luminaries from Winneba and Senya Beraku, Ghana

Charles Blankson

XULON PRESS

Xulon Press
2301 Lucien Way #415
Maitland, FL 32751
407.339.4217
www.xulonpress.com

Paperback ISBN-13: 978-1-6628-4727-1
Ebook ISBN-13: 978-1-6628-4766-0

The Author

Charles Codman Taylor Blankson, Ph.D.

C harles Blankson was born in Winneba, Ghana on 12th June, 1944. His parents were Oman Ghan Blankson and Jane NaYɛNa Arthur. His father is featured in this book. Charles is the eighth of eleven children. He was educated at the Winneba Methodist Primary and Middle Schools and at Mfantsipim Secondary School in Cape Coast. He had his sixth-form education at Presbyterian Secondary School at Odumase Krobo and obtained his bachelor's degree in economics at the University of Ghana, Legon, in 1968. He got his master's degree in regional planning from the Kwame Nkrumah University of Science and Technology (KNUST), Kumasi, in 1970, and earned a doctorate in urban and regional planning from the University of California, Los Angeles (UCLA) in 1989.

After obtaining his master's degree, he worked as a research fellow at the Housing and Planning Research Department in the Faculty of Architecture at KNUST from 1971 through 1980, before proceeding to UCLA for his doctorate. Charles taught urban planning part-time at the California State University at Northridge during the 1987/88 academic year and worked for two years at the Southern California Association of Governments in Los Angeles after graduating from UCLA. He retired in 2008 from the South Coast Air Quality Management District in Diamond Bar, California, as an environmental planner, after nearly 18 years with the agency.

Charles has published seven articles on urban and regional development planning for developing countries in academic journals and produced two family tree reports, one covering his father and the other his mother. He has one United States patent for an automobile visor. Charles is also a musician, having sung in choirs since eleven years old, and a Christian since his first year at the University of Ghana, Legon, in 1966.

Charles was organist at Legon Hall Chapel at the University of Ghana, Legon, (1966 – 1968). He was organist and assistant choir director, and choir director at the University non-denominational (Protestant) Chaplaincy at the Kwame Nkrumah University of Science and Technology, Kumasi, from 1969 – 1980. While in Southern California, he has sung in the choir at the Culver-Palms United Methodist Church in Culver City, and served as choir director at United Methodist Churches in Rancho Cucamonga (1992 – 1998), and Arlington in Riverside (2004 – 2017). He is currently the choir director at the Moreno Valley United Methodist Church. He has composed over 50 hymn tunes.

Apart from his family, friends and church, Charles's greatest satisfaction and passion is his involvement in the Awutu-Effutu and Friends Association of Southern California (AEFASC). The association is made up of persons who were born and grew up in Winneba and Senya Beraku but are currently living in Southern California. The Association also has "Friends" as members. These are individuals who are Ghanaians with no association to either town, but are inspired by the goals of the association. They believe that any improvement in any part of the country goes to the benefit of the entire country, helping raise their standards of living.

The Association has been engaged in the shipment of essential hospital supplies, (including X-ray equipment and drill bits), to the Winneba Hospital over the years. The association's other most notable projects included renovating the buildings of the Winneba Methodist Primary School buildings during the early 2000s. It also provided financial assistance to the Ark-City Link Foundation, an institution, founded and run by Tom and Felicity Archurst, that provides basic computer skills to elementary school children and their teachers in Winneba. Most recently, the association has sponsored seven students to get into colleges and universities in Ghana. Charles believes that to whom that much is given, much is expected. He feels the need to give back to a country that has given him so much. Charles has been president of the association for well over 20 years.

Charles currently lives in Southridge, a suburb of Fontana, in Southern California with his wife, Sophia, of 46 years. They have three children, Ekua Walker, Araba Mensah and Koby Blankson, and five grandchildren, Qiana Elizabeth Walker, Bright Ato Mensah, Evans Kofi Mensah, Kaya Sophia Walker and Charles Blankson Mensah.

The author and Family

Preface

The idea to write this book originated in late December 2020 while I was listening to my daughter, Ekua NaYεNa Walker, interviewing my niece, Awo Quaison-Sackey, on Ekua's podcast www.momschangingtheworld.org. Awo was talking about her late father, Alex Quaison-Sackey, who had been Ghana's ambassador to the United Nations Organization (UN) during the late 1950s and later Ghana's foreign minister in the 1960s. Awo described the incredible life of her father. Some of this information was new to me, someone fairly close to Alex as a brother-in-law.

Three thoughts occurred to me while I was listening to this interview. The first was that there were many people, like Alex, who had risen to the top of their respective careers, and had made significant contributions to the life of the country and beyond. The second was that these were people who had connections with Winneba, and Senya Beraku. These individuals were either born or raised in these two towns. Winneba is about 50 km. west of Accra and Senya Beraku about 30 km. west of Accra. These thoughts were intriguing and needed to be explored. The third and perhaps the most important thought was that their lives might have lessons that could serve as inspiration to those who may not have known about their achievements. Their stories needed to be told and shared beyond what was known to just a few. The idea I had was that with passing generations, what these people did and achieved had important life changing lessons that would be lost, if not documented. Books may be written about each Individual but to have the highlights of their lives all assembled in one book would be invaluable.

William George Tarrant, the 19th Century hymnist, said it best when he wrote about the need to praise great and famous men and women, the fathers and mothers named in history: paraphrasing: the wise, the brave and strong, who helped the right and fought the wrong, men and women, great of heart and mind, singers greatly gifted, whose music, like a mighty wind, uplifted the souls of people, the powerful men and women of skill who built homes of beauty, those rich in art, who made richer still the "brotherhood of duty." God revealed His glory through the lives of all these famous people that we all revere.

Throughout history, men and women have emerged who have made significant contributions to improve human lives. There are those whose ideas helped change and shape the world for the better in different ways. By their ideas or concepts, some helped mold and organize societies, and some created objects and systems that have improved lives from primitive levels to higher levels of productivity, convenience and comfort.

The following come to mind: Philosophers like Plato and Aristotle; artists like Leonardo da Vinci, Rembrandt van Rijn, Pierre Auguste Renoir and Michelangelo Buonarroti; musicians like Wolfgang Amadeus Mozart, Johann Sebastian Bach, Ludwig van Beethoven, Frantz Peter Schubert, Johannes Brahms, Franz Joseph Haydn and George Frideric Handel; writers like William Shakespeare and Thomas Hardy; scientists like Galileo Galilei, Nicolaus Copernicus and Albert Einstein, and lastly inventors and visionaries like Henry Ford, Bette Nesmith Graham (Liquid Paper), Ruth Handler (Barbie Dolls), Shirley Chinery (Geographic Positioning Systems), Grace Murray Hopper (COBOL- Common Business-Oriented Language for computers), Mary Anderson (Windshield Wipers), William Henry (Bill) Gates III, Steven Paul Jobs, Bill Hewlett, David Packard, Stephen Gary (Steve) Wozniak,

Jeffrey Preston (Jeff) Bezos, to name a few. Those mentioned earlier lived hundreds of years ago, but we still remember their works.

The small coastal towns of Winneba and Senya Beraku in Ghana have produced men and women who have made significant achievements in their lives. I can identify three groups of people who were born and raised in Winneba and Senya Beraku who have made names for themselves and contributed in significant ways to the life of the country.

The first group includes persons well known on the international stage: Alex Quaison-Sackey became president of the United Nations General Assembly and later Ghana's foreign minister. Kow Nkensen Arkaah was Ghana's Vice-president. Professors Joseph Yanney Ewusie, Kwesi Abotsia Dickson and Kwamena Busumafi Dickson wrote books that were used as text books in schools and colleges not only in Ghana but elsewhere in Africa. Professor Albert Morgan Wright developed the Kumasi Ventilated Improvement Pit Latrine (KVIPL), starting from Reid's Odorless Earth Closet used in South Africa. This new and improved system continues to be used throughout rural Africa.

The second group includes persons well known within the Country: Oman Ghan Blankson for his music compositions, Robert Herbert Blankson for his business and entrepreneurial spirit, the Jacksons for their excellence in the teaching of mathematics and engineering, the Sams for diplomacy and engineering, Kweku Budu Manuel, Kweku Ghartey-Tagoe, Kobena Taylor, and Kodwo Halm for radio and television broadcasting.

The third but by no means the least important are persons who were well known within the town: William Freebody Acquah who wrote musicals and cantatas for the Winneba Methodist Church, Mr. Asibu who owned a modern brewery, A. W. Yamoah who owned a hardware store, Mr. Samuel Kwesi Ansah Ghartey who owned a store interestingly named "All British Goods", Kow Sawyer, K. B. Annan and Charles Acquaah who were building contractors.

All these mentioned and many more are persons whose stories need to be told for posterity. The generations that know about their achievements are nearly gone.

Not all of these persons mentioned above, and others I wanted to profile but not mentioned, are covered in this book. Thankfully, many of those I contacted were enthusiastic about the project and were willing to offer information about themselves. Some were also willing to get information about those I had asked about that they knew. A few of those I contacted declined to be involved.

I used several sources in gathering information for this book. Regarding those who are alive at the time of writing, most of the information came from the individuals themselves. Most of the information for those who are deceased came from three main sources. One was from publications by family to celebrate their lives at their passing. The second source was their children and others who knew them. The third source was information that was in the public domain, such as interviews, books and articles. For example, information on Brigadier General Joseph Nunoo-Mensah came mostly from interviews that he has given over the years. For those, including Nunoo-Mensah, whose lives were impacted by their involvement in government and politics, their information came from books, manuscripts and articles.

The biographies run from a few paragraphs for some to several pages for others. The person with the shortest biography is William Freebody-Acquah, whom I knew as a great musician when I was growing up. He was a natural musician, not having received any formal music training. He improvised musicals that were performed by groups in the Winneba Methodist Church. Sadly, there was little or no information about him anywhere. Being a musician myself and having composed a little over 50 simple hymn tunes and knowing how difficult it is to do even that, I cannot imagine how challenging it must have been for him to compose musicals, complete with narration and heart-warming melodies.

You are talking about a "Miranda Lin Manuel" (of the Broadway musical "Hamilton" fame) of yesteryear and not even a page of history has been written about his life. This absence of an essential part of the town's music history is one of the reasons why this book is important.

The goal of this book is to inspire the current and future generations of Ghanaians through learning about the backgrounds and lives of these greats and how they became who they were. The main lesson is that it does not matter how poor or rich, how educated or uneducated a person's parents are, success in life is possible. Some of the persons covered in this book were spotted by their teachers or senior relatives who saw the potential in them and nurtured them. All of them were simply brilliant and grew up in environments that enabled them to thrive.

As an aside, the question that comes to mind is how Winneba and Senya Beraku came to produce such eminent scholars, professionals and entrepreneurs. One of the key factors is colonialism. Colonialism, simply defined, is a system by which a nation controls other nations or peoples. Part of this system is a process that draws the colonized people and country into a global economy through which the colonized are exploited by the colonizers. Winneba played a key role in that process.

Winneba, unlike Accra or Cape Coast, had a deep natural harbor. Ships loaded with agricultural products like cocoa, rubber and palm oil for export, would dock a mile away at sea. The local fishermen would row their boats with the cargo of these agricultural raw materials meant for export to the ships. After unloading their cargo onto the ships, the boats would be reloaded with imported items like rice, flour, sugar, chocolate, corned beef, sardines, ice cream, apples, potatoes, books and others that would be rowed back to shore. This export and import of goods through Winneba started during the late 1880s and continued until the new port of Tema was built near Accra in the early 1960s.

Most of this export and import trading was carried out by foreign companies. Famous among these companies were the United Africa Company which had been preceded by Messrs Millers & Company, G. B. Ollivant, Union Trading Company, Cadbury Brothers, East Trading Company, Commonwealth Trust Limited, Societe' Commerciale de L'Ouest Africaine, Compagnie Francaise de L'Afrique Occidentale, John Holt Bartholomew Limited and Patterson Zochonnis Limited. These companies built huge warehouses all over town to house the products for the goods awaiting shipment to sea. The warehouses also served as repositories for the imported items that were later driven for distribution for sale to the rest of the country.

In order to produce the clerks that would help process the volumes of goods to be exported and imported, schools, mostly elementary and middle, were established all over town. Interestingly enough, the schools were established not by the trading companies but by the Christian missionaries, predominantly Catholics, Methodists, Presbyterians and Anglicans. It is not clear whether there was any collaboration between the trading companies and the missionaries. However, the work of the missionaries played a significant role in helping produce the staff that was needed by the trading companies. Later on, the Winneba Local Council also added their own schools. Parents were encouraged to send their children to school to prepare them for careers with these companies. The benefits from being "educated" were quite obvious. One was being able to live like their white superiors. The expected higher living conditions were undeniably much better than those of their parents, who were mostly fishermen and market women engaged in retail fishing in local markets. In sum, however, despite the negative connotations associated with colonialism, it is fair to say that the colonial system worked very efficiently by laying the infrastructure that made Winneba what it was and enabled the town to produce the luminaries covered in this book.

The book is divided into four main sections. The first section, the Internationals, covers politicians, diplomats and a professional. The second section, the Academicians, covers those whose careers revolved around the universities. The third section, the Professionals, is almost a misnomer since every successful person is a professional in his or her field. This title is maintained for lack of a better classification. The fourth and last section, the Next Generation, covers children of those first generation achievers who have carried on the tradition of success started by their parents. This last section covers just a few of these professionals just to illustrate a trend. This is because once the benefits of education became widely known, the individuals, who had achieved success in their various areas, gave their children the opportunities that allowed them to succeed. Most of their children have become successful professionals as well. It has become like a tree, growing almost exponentially, with branches, with each succeeding generation.

In writing this book, it became clear that there are overlaps resulting from persons whose professions blossomed both at home and abroad and were recognized as such. However, one thing that is common to all four groups of people is the fact that they all rose to the highest levels in their areas of profession. The order of reporting within each group is based roughly on age.

The reader will notice that the dates are written with the day first, followed by the month and the year. This is the format used in Ghana where this book is positioned. There are also spelling differences in words like honors for honours and program for programme.

Sources for Ghana's Political History

Frempong, Alexander K. D. (2007) "Political Conflict and Elite Consensus in the Liberal State" in Ghana: One Decade of the Liberal State, ed. Kwame Boafo-Arthur, Council for the Development of Social Science Research in Africa, (CODESRIA), Dakar, pp. 128 – 164.

Owusu, Maxwell (1996) "Tradition and Transformation: Democracy and the Politics of Popular Power in Ghana" in The Journal of Modern African Studies, 34, 2, pp. 307 – 343.

Ghana Government: Ghana National Reconciliation Commission Report, Vol. 4, Ch. 1, "The Security Services" (October 2004).

"Ghana, Life After Jerry", The Economist, December 2, 2000, pg. 47.

"Governance: 100 Days of Peaceful Revolution – An Analysis of the Kuffuor Presidency" The Ghanaian Chronicle, Vol. 9, No. 100, April 26, 2001.

Ade Sawyerr (2019), "Relevance of Nkrumah's Vision for Ghana and Africa" in https://adesawyerr.wordpress.com, September 28.

March 2022

Acknowledgments

T he author owes a great debt of gratitude to the following persons without whose help this book would not have been possible:

Professor Ebenezer Asafua Jackson, Professor John Humphrey Amuasi and Mr. Kwesi Abbey Sam for going beyond the call of duty to provide information beyond their own lives. Professor Amuasi's help has been invaluable throughout the entire process through to marketing the book. I am eternally grateful to him. Mr. Joe Baiden-Amissah and Mr. John Hanson Howard for pointing me to persons whose achievements needed to be celebrated.

Mr. David Tenenbaum, the "people's librarian" in Chicago provided guidance on funding sources and the copyright process.

Dr. Emmanuel Annor, Rev. John Annan Dadzie and Dr. Waldo Lopez-Aqueres provided critical editorial comments. Dr. Lopez-Aqueres also provided a review and a recommendation.

Araba and Ishmael Bright Mensah, my daughter and her husband, provided computer technical assistance whenever I got lost and didn't know what to do. Beyond simple emailing and creating Word documents, the two have taught me almost everything else I now know about computers. At the beginning of the father-son-in-law technological relationship years ago, Ishmael inserted hardware that expanded my computer memory. He also massaged the pictures to meet the current publisher's print quality requirements for this book. The latest they taught me was the placement of the pictures in the text. I am grateful to Araba for designing the cover page.

Finally, Sophia, my wife, suggested persons to be included in the book and also came up with the idea to include pictures of the profiled to give a human face and touch to the book. Sophia continues to inspire and support me in all my endeavors.

Dedication

This book is dedicated to Paapa, Maame, Sophia, Ekua, Araba, Koby, Quentin, Ishmael, Olga, Qiana, Bright, Evans, Kaya and Charlie.

Foreward

David Tenenbaum

My interest in Ghana and Osagyefo Dr. Kwame Nkrumah began with my studies in African politics at the University of California Los Angeles (UCLA) in the early 1970s. I met Charles, then a graduate student, by chance at the UCLA Research Library. We both got off an elevator and I looked at his Ghana Airways flight bag and began to ask, "Are you from…" and before I could finish the sentence he said, "Yes." Thus began a remarkable friendship that has lasted, dare I say, over half a century.

Dr. Blankson has painstakingly assembled a timeless collection of profiles that will both educate and inspire the reader. From history-making diplomats to university professors and beyond, this book describes the conditions that enabled two seaside towns to produce such luminaries.

Read this book and you will be amazed if not inspired, by how, from very humble beginnings these lives were transformed. Education is vital and transformational. One thing is for sure. No trip to Ghana is complete without a visit to Winneba and Senya Beraku.

TABLE OF CONTENTS

Section A – The Internationals 1

1. Mr. Alex Quaison-Sackey 3
2. Mr. Kow Nkensen Arkaah 10
3. Mr. Kweku Ghartey Sam, Sr. 14
4. Mr. Josiah Wobil 19

Section B – The Academicians 25

1. Professor Joseph Yanney Ewusie 27
2. Most Rev. Prof. Kwesi Abotsia Dickson 33
3. Mr. Christopher John Yarney 37
4. Professor Daniel Kwamena Abbiw-Jackson 41
5. Mr. Joseph Samuel Gyakye Jackson 46
6. Professor George Kwamena Tetteh 49
7. Professor Osborne Augustus Yamoah Jackson 52
8. Professor Daniel Afedzi Akyeampong 56
9. Professor Henry Walter Richardson 61
10. Professor Ebenezer Asafua Jackson 68
11. Professor Albert Ebo Richardson 75
12. Professor John Humphrey Amuasi 83

Section C – The Professionals. 91

1. Mr. Sam Mensah Herbert Baxter Yarney 93
2. Mr. Oman Ghan Blankson 96
3. Mr. William Freebody Acquah. 100
4. Mr. Robert Herbert Blankson 101
5. Mr. Samuel Andoh Bannerman. 103
6. Mrs. Elsie Quaison-Sackey. 105
7. Mr. Mark Kweku Budu-Manuel 108
8. Mr. David Kweku Ghartey-Tagoe 111
9. Mrs. Efua Amakyewa Mills-Robertson 116
10. Mr. Kweku Sagoe Sam 120
11. Brigadier General Joseph Nunoo-Mensah (Rtd.). 122
12. Colonel Kofi Abaka Jackson (Rtd.). 131
13. Mr. Kwesi Abbey Sam. 135
14. Mr. Joseph Ebow Bannerman 141
15. Mrs. Felicity Efua Arkhurst. 148
16. Rt. Rev. Dr. Joseph Kow Ghunney 151

Section D – The Next Generation. 155

1. Mr. Harvey Gyansa Essilfie. 157
2. Professor Ruby Hanson 160
3. Dr. Kweku Ghartey Sam, Jr. 165

Epilogue. 169

Section A

The Internationals

Mr. Alex Quaison Sackey

Early Years and Education

Alex was born on 9th August, 1924, to Alexander Emmanuel Sackey (Kweku Sekyi) of Winneba and Alberta Ekua Kwesiwa Quaison from Ewusiedwo in the Ahanta District of the Western Region. Alex came from a royal line going back to Nana Acquah I of Winneba, in the early 1900s. Alex's paternal uncle was Nana Ayirebi Acquah III who was chief of Winneba during the 1940s to early 1950s. At Alex's outdooring, he was named in honor of his grandfather, Kodwo Sei. Kodwo stands for a son born on Monday, although Alex was born on a Saturday which would traditionally have made him Kwame or Kwamena.

After completing his middle school education at the Winneba Methodist Middle School with distinction, Alex was admitted to

3

Mfantsipim Secondary School in Cape Coast in 1940. He was head prefect in his final year, 1945. The head prefect, in almost all secondary schools, was usually an outstanding final year student. Alex had the privilege of delivering the student leader's address at the Speech and Prize-Giving Day. His eloquence and voice tone charmed the audience. Many could tell that day that Alex was destined to be a leader and a public figure.

Alex passed the school certificate examination with distinction and exemption from London Matriculation. He attended Achimota Secondary School from 1946 through 1948. Mfantsipim didn't have the sixth form at the time so students who passed their final examinations were sent to Achimota to do the sixth form. After graduating from Achimota, Alex was admitted to Exeter College, Oxford University, in October 1949, on a Gold Coast Government scholarship. Alex graduated from Oxford in 1952 with honors in Politics, Philosophy and Economics (P.P.E.) which Oxonians call "Modern Greats". The bachelor's degree was subsequently advanced to the master's degree in the Oxford University tradition.

Career Path

On his return to the Gold Coast early 1950s, Alex joined the civil service and was posted to Tarkwa as a labor officer. In 1955, he was selected along with seven others by the Public Services Commission to train as diplomats for the country's future diplomatic corps. They were known as Trainee Foreign Service Officers. The eight trainees were sent to the London School of Economics for a six-month course in international law, relations and economics. His first foreign service posting was to the British Embassy in Rio de Janeiro, Brazil, in 1956.

Alex's first major diplomatic engagement was in 1957 when he was appointed a member of the Ghana delegation to the meeting of the General Agreement on Tariffs and Trade (GATT). In

4

the same year he was posted to the High Commission in London as Second Secretary. One of his assignments as Second Secretary was to act as liaison officer between the Ghana Mission and the other African Missions in London for the preparatory work for the first Conference of Independent African States which was scheduled for Accra in April 1958. In 1959, Alex was appointed Ghana's permanent representative to the United Nations with concurrent accreditation to Cuba and Mexico. The following year, he was made president of the General Assembly. The presidency is a one year position that rotates among member states.

Alex's eloquence, persuasiveness and sharp leadership qualities were noticed by the leadership of the United Nations. He was subsequently made a member of several committees. He was appointed chairman of the United Nations Committee on Information from Non-Self-Governing Territories. In 1960, he was made a member of the Committee of Experts for the Re-Organization of the United Nations Secretariat. He was also appointed a member of the United Nations Conciliation Commission to the Congo.

Alex was appointed vice-president of the United Nations General Assembly at its 16th Regular Session for the 1961-1962 session. Ghana was elected to serve a two-year term (1962-63) on the United Nations Security Council. Alex became Africa's spokesman on the Security Council. Incidentally, he presided over the Security Council twice during Ghana's two-year tenure of office.

Alex was appointed a member of the Ghana Delegation to the Conference of Independent African States held in Addis Ababa in 1963. It was at this Addis Ababa conference that the Organization of African Unity (OAU) now African Union (AU) was formed. Alex was a member of the drafting committee of the Organization's Charter. With Kwame Nkrumah's high profile on the international stage fighting for the independence of the still colonized parts of Africa, the OAU became the driving force behind the decolonization of the rest of Africa. Alex was nominated by the African Group and elected by the General Assembly to the prestigious position of President of the 19th Regular Session of the United Nations General Assembly for the 1964-65 session. He became the first African, South of the Sahara, to hold that office. As president, he also chaired the United Nations Committee of Thirteen on Peace-Keeping Operations.

Post 1966

In 1965, Alex was invited home by President Kwame Nkrumah and became a member of parliament for Enyan Breman and subsequently Ghana's Foreign Minister. It was during his tenure as foreign minister, on his way to Hanoi on 24 February, 1966, with Kwame Nkrumah to help resolve the Vietnam War that Nkrumah's administration was overthrown by the country's armed forces. Alex returned to Ghana soon after the coup hoping to continue serving the country he loved dearly. He saw himself as a technocrat and therefore apolitical. The military junta thought otherwise. The junta saw him as a politician and a member of Nkrumah's outlawed Convention Peoples Party. Alex was arrested and sent to Ussher Fort Prisons in Accra, where he was kept in a cell, a political prisoner.

After his release from prison a year later, Alex proceeded to London where, after completing his law studies, he was called to the bar by the Honorable Society of Lincoln's Inn in July 1969. On his return to Ghana later that year, he registered as a barrister and solicitor of the Superior Court of Judicature. He practiced law briefly with the chambers of Lynes Quarshie-Idun and Company in Accra. In October 1970, he left Lynes Quarshie-Idun and Company and set up his own law office with his friend, E. B. Okai Anderson. They named their company Sackandah Chambers, which was made up from their last names, Sackey and Anderson.

However, in 1978, twelve years after the military coup, the Supreme Military Council, under the chairmanship of Lieutenant-General F. W. K. Akuffo, recognizing Alex's immense fame as a diplomat and a statesman along with his elegance in language and disposition, appointed him as Ghana's ambassador to the United States with accreditation to Mexico. He served in that capacity until 1980. In 1988, he joined the executive staff of Japan Motors Company in Accra as general manager and legal director. In January 1991, he and four other Ghanaians were appointed Goodwill Ambassadors by the Ghana Red Cross Society to support the World Campaign for the Protection of Victims of War.

Life as a Methodist

Alex was raised a Christian. In high school, he joined the Mfantsipim Evangelical Group and would go with fellow students on Sundays to conduct worship services at Antem and Ekon, small villages outside Cape Coast. While at Achimota Secondary School, Alex was president of the Student Christian Movement. When he settled at home after his diplomatic career ended, he became very active in the Ghana Methodist Conference. He served on the Church's General Purposes Council, the Church's highest governing and legislative body.

Alex served as Vice-President of the Ghana Methodist Conference in 1985-87. He also served on the Constitution Review Committee which produced the Church's Revised Constitution that was adopted by the General Conference of 1989. When he returned to Britain to study for the bar, he worshipped at the Methodist Church at Golders Green, near London.

On the ecumenical scene, Alex served on various committees of the Christian Council of Ghana and the All Africa Conference of Churches. His last ecumenical involvement was as a member of the Sixth Assembly of the All Africa Conference of Churches in Harare, Zimbabwe from October 25 – 29, 1992.

Awards

He was awarded several honorary doctors of law degrees by universities in the United States of America. A few are Montclair State University in 1965, the University of California Berkley in 1965 and the University of Cincinnati in 1978.

Civic Life

Alex also had time for his home community of Winneba. He was appointed a member of the Effutu Traditional Council and was the Council's legal advisor. In that capacity, Alex led all the Council's delegations in their interactions with the Central Regional and National Council of Chiefs and the government. Alex was a Freemason and remained an active member of the Lodge throughout his life. He was initiated into Warsaw Lodge, No. 7141 under the Register of the United Grand Lodge of England in June 1955.

Following after that Alex was either a member or a founding member of several Lodges. These included Winneba Lodge, Chapter No. 7708, Public Service Lodge No. 8587, Mfantsipim Lodge No. 7260, Orbis Lodge No. 9334, Meridian Lodge of Installed Masters No. 9386, and Volta Chapter No. 8652. He also served as President of the District Board of Benevolence. The following are some of the highlights of his involvement: He became a member of the Progressive Lodge, No. 11662 in Winneba in 1976. He was promoted to Past Noble Father a year later, and then a member of the Perpetual Household of Ruth No. 1213 of Winneba. He was admitted into the Council Maters' Chapter No. 1 months later. He became Vice-Grand Master of Progressive Lodge in Winneba in

1985. In 1986, he was promoted to Most Noble Grand Master. In 1987, he was appointed to the Central District Lodge No. 1, and became District Master of the Lodge in 1989.

Family

Alex and the former Elsie Annie Blankson were married in 1951, while both were students in London. They were married at the Norwich Methodist Church. They were blessed with six children; Egya Akumbia (psychiatrist), Nana Bɔdɔ (lawyer), Awo Aferba (lawyer), Kweku Bondze Asiedu (business administrator) Nenyi Kweku Embi (sound engineer and guitar bassist), and Yaaba (lawyer). His hobbies were reading, listening to jazz and classical music, singing hymns, and playing tennis and card games. He was a good man. He had time for everyone, big or small. He was gregarious, and loved hanging out with family and friends over good food and drinks. He passed into eternity on December 21, 1992, at the age of 68, leaving behind Elsie, his wife of 41 years, five children and three grandchildren.

Mr. K. B. Ayensu, a colleague and a very good friend, gave a moving eulogy at Alex's funeral. He referred to Alex as one of several Alexanders who had achieved tremendous success and greatness in their time. The first Alexander was Alexander the Great who, at the time of his death at 33, had conquered most of the Eastern world. Mr. Ayensu went on to list five Catholic popes, three Russian czars, and a king of Yugoslavia, all of whom were called Alexander. Lastly, there was Earl Alexander of Tunis, who was a great military strategist during World War II. Mr. Ayensu's remarks were a fitting tribute to a man who was destined to achieve greatness and did so. Alex's 1963 book, "Africa Unbound" had a subtitle, "The Reflections of an African Statesman". A statesman indeed!

Mr. Kow Nkensen Arkaah

Early Life and Education

M r. Kow Arkaah was born on 14th July, 1927, at Senya Beraku. His parents were John Kweku Arkaah, Tufuhene of Senya Beraku and Adwoa Apaade Johnson, also from Senya Beraku. Kow's mother was also from a royal house headed by her father, Nenyi Issiw II. Kow's father traded in imported goods and had stores in Senya, Winneba, Agona Swedru, Accra and Keta. Kow started his education at the Methodist School in 1936 and completed in 1941. He attended Mfantsipim Secondary School from 1941 through 1946, then did the sixth form at Achimota Secondary School. Kow got admission to Lincoln University in 1948, then transferred to Tufts University (1950 – 1952), where he earned his bachelor's degree. Kow continued on to Harvard University (1952 – 1954) where he got his MBA.

Career Path

Mr. Arkaah started his professional career as assistant sales manager at Secony Oil Company in New York. On his return to Ghana in 1955, he worked with Mobil Oil Company as a marketing executive through 1957. He joined the Ministry of Trade within the Ghana Civil Service in 1958, and was promoted from one position to another until he became Principal Secretary in 1965. He served as chief executive officer of Ghana Industrial Holding Corporation (GIHOC) from 1966 – 1968, Supervising Principal Secretary at the Ministry of Foreign Affairs, 1968 – 1969, and general manager of Ghana National Trading Corporation (GNTC) 1969 – 1972. Under his leadership, GNTC established retail outlets all over the country.

Mr. Arkaah was appointed managing director of Ghana Airways in 1973 and chief executive of Ghana National Procurement Agency (1978 – 1979). As chief commercial officer for foreign trade in the Ministry of Trade, Mr. Arkaah helped set up retail stores in the Gambia, Sierra Leone, Yugoslavia and Ethiopia, all based on the GNTC model. Upon retiring from the public service, Mr. Arkaah set up a consultancy that worked for the government of Yugoslavia in 1979, Johnson Products USA in 1982 – 1983, the government of Ethiopia in 1984, and the government of Lesotho from 1986 – 1988. Mr. Arkaah was appointed managing director of Ghana Oil Company (GOIL), where he served until 1992.

Civic Life and Politics

Mr. Arkaah was interested in local chieftaincy as well. He followed in his father's footsteps when he was enstooled as Tufuhene of Senya Beraku in 1973, with the stool name Nenyi Kow Nkensen

I. Working at the local town level and interacting with the government led to an interest in national politics. In 1979 Mr. Arkaah joined the People's National Party (PNP) and won the parliamentary seat representing the Awutu-Effutu-Senya constituency. In parliament, he was elected chairman of the Parliamentary Select Committee on Trade, Industries, Tourism, Science and Technology.

Mr. Arkaah's foray into national politics* saw him as the vice-presidential running mate to John Agyekum Kuffuor, heading an alliance of Nkrumah's Convention Peoples Party and J. B. Danquah / K. A. Busia's New Patriotic Party. He joined the National Convention Party (NCP) in 1990, and later got into an alliance with the Every Ghanaian Living Everywhere (EGLE) Party and National Democratic Congress (NDC) with Flight Lieutenant Jerry John Rawlings as the head. When the NDC and allied parties won the 1992 general elections, Jerry Rawlings became president and Arkaah became his vice-president. Their relationship was quite fractious.

While serving as the vice-president of the country with Jerry Rawlings as president, Arkaah became leader of the Convention People's Party (CPP). The CPP was a merger of the National Convention Party (NCP) and People's Convention Party (PCP). This merger was formed on 29th January, 1996. Arkaah went on to make history when, still as vice-president to President Jerry Rawlings, he stood as presidential candidate for the Convention People's Party for the 1996 general elections. Arkaah's Convention Peoples Party lost the elections. Arkaah was replaced by John Atta Mills as President Jerry Rawlings' vice-president.

Hobbies

Mr. Arkaah's hobbies were singing, reading, and gardening. He started singing in the Winneba Methodist Church Choir when he was in middle school. His love for music led him to be a founding patron for the Winneba Youth Choir.

Family

Mr. Arkaah was married in 1963 to the former Marian Riberio Ayeh. They were blessed with five children, three girls, Bentuma, Yaaba and Preba and two boys, Kofi Ayeh Nkensen and Ato Yaabeni.

Arkaah was seriously injured in a vehicle accident at Cantonments in Accra and died of those injuries in Atlanta, Georgia, in the United States on 25 April, 2001, at age 74.

*Source on Politics: Frempong, Alexander K. D. (2007), "Political Conflict and Elite Consensus in the Liberal State", in Kwame Boafo-Arthur (ed.) Ghana: One Decade of the Liberal State, Council for the Development of Social Science Research in Africa (CODESRIA), Dakar, pp 128 – 164.

Mr. Kweku Ghartey Sam, Snr.

Early Life and Education

Kweku Ghartey Sam was born on Wednesday, 12th April, 1933, in Winneba. His parents were Mr. Robert James Sam popularly known as Brother Sam, and the former Grace Andam (Maame Ekuwa Kwegyirba), also from Winneba. Kweku's father, R. J. Sam, was a catechist and local preacher in the Winneba Methodist Church. The mother was a homemaker. Kweku was the third child and one of seven siblings of his parents. He was named Kweku Gyɛtɛ and later Christened Kweku Ghartey Sam. Three of his siblings, Efua Amakyewa Mills-Robertson, Sagoe Sam and Kwesi Abbey Sam, are profiled elsewhere in this book.

K. G., as he was fondly called by his siblings, wife, family and friends, attended the Winneba Methodist Primary and Senior

Schools from 1938 to 1948. After completing Standard Seven, he went to Kumasi to live with his paternal uncle, Mr. Jacob Antobam Sackey, a tutor at Wesley College. In Kumasi, he taught as a pupil-teacher for one year before entering Wesley College in January 1950, to train as a Certificate 'A' teacher.

During his first year as a teacher, K. G. prepared Standard 6 pupils for the Common Entrance Examination. One of his pupils was his younger brother, Kwesi Abbey Sam, who passed the examination and entered Mfantsipim Secondary School in January 1955. K. G. himself did not have the opportunity to go to secondary school. However, soon after starting teaching, he studied privately, sat and passed the General Certificate of Education, Ordinary and Advanced levels, in June 1956 and June 1957 respectively.

After graduating from Wesley College in December 1953, K. G. was posted to the Winneba Methodist School with other newly minted teachers from Winneba. These were Henry Acquah Mills-Robertson, who was posted to Methodist Middle Boys School, Mrs. Hagar Hazel, nee' Hagar Parry, and Mrs. Elizabeth Acquah Sampson, nee' Elizabeth Ayirebi-Acquah, the latter both posted to the Methodist Girls School. The four became lifelong friends. He also took some overseas correspondence courses in economics, then got a diploma in public administration at the Ghana Institute of Management and Public Administration in 1976.

Career Path

K.G. joined the civil service in 1959, and was assigned to the Ministry of External Affairs. From 1960 to 1963, he served as the 3rd and 2nd Secretary at the Embassy of Ghana in Tokyo, Japan. He returned to the ministry in Accra where he served from 1963 until 1966. He was then posted to Bamako, Mali, as the Charge d'Affaires and later Head of Chancery at the Embassy of Ghana in Mali from 1966 to 1968. Between 1970 and 1974, he was the

Director of Passport Division at the Ministry of Foreign Affairs. The Ghana government, at the time, was having difficulty placing the young professionals in the civil service so it introduced a benefits and incentives program under which those who had served in government for some years could retire. K.G. took advantage of that program and retired in 1976.

Entrepreneurship and Business

K.G. was quite an entrepreneur. He took advantage of his retirement to put his entrepreneurial talents to work. He was willing to take risks so he invested in a variety of enterprises. He started with a poultry farm, a few miles outside Winneba. Experimenting with products from the poultry farm led his mother to develop 'Grace Sausage', a delicacy which the family heartily enjoyed at Abandze Fie, the family home.

K. G. next went into the transportation business. He started with a taxi, then a mini-van that had the inscription 'Adze Nyinara Bɔbɔ Adze, Ɔbeka Onyame Nkoaa', meaning "all human endeavors will cease except God's." K.G. and his siblings founded a construction company, Brosam Limited, specializing in the construction of roads and bridges. He served as an executive member of the Ghana Construction Association. He was also a member of the national executive council of the Association of Road Contractors.

K. G.'s other projects included running a motel for the general public and a hostel for students at the University of Education, Winneba. He was an avid golfer and belonged to the Achimota Golf Club. He built a nine-hole golf course which he called the Windy Bay Golf Links adjacent to the poultry farm. The golf course hosted golf tournaments at least once yearly during the first weekend in May, when the town's Deer Hunt festival was celebrated. The GyeteKrom property currently has an apartment complex that has been rented out to the Police Department. At some point, K. G.

also owned a fishing boat which he operated in partnership with one of the local fishermen at Teshie Nungua near Accra. These many enterprises showed his commitment to the economic development of the town and beyond since they provided jobs for the young men and women in the area.

Benevolence

K. G. was a very charitable man. This trait led him to start a scholarship program that was run through the Winneba Methodist Church. The scholarships were meant for students who had gained admission to any tertiary institution in the country. Since his passing, this program has been taken up graciously by his children. The current scholarship beneficiary is in her final year at the University of Education, Winneba, and is planning to go into teaching upon graduation.

Politics

In politics, K.G. had great fondness for Ghana's first president, Kwame Nkrumah, as most young people did during the First Republic. During the Third Republic under Fl. Lt. Jerry John Rawlings, from 1992 through 2008, K. G. was active in the Peoples National Party at the local level. The early weeks and months of Rawling's June 1981 coup were chaotic. Anybody who had achieved anything in life and was successful was seen as a potential enemy of the revolution. So even though he was neither a member of parliament nor a minister in government, K. G. and other senior personnel and successful business persons were arrested and taken to Nsawam Prison, Cantonments Police Station and Police Headquarters Annex for interrogation.

K. G. was acquitted after several inquiries were conducted into his businesses and they found nothing incriminatory in his business dealings and enterprises. In the Fourth Republic under John Agyekum Kuffuor, K.G. joined the New Patriotic Party and was very active in Winneba, serving as one of the party's elders.

Life as a Methodist

Throughout his life, K. G. served the Lord with all his heart and strength. Like his parents, K. G. lived his life in the church. He served as a chorister and in various positions from the society level to the Conference (national) level. On 27th August, 2012, he was admitted to the Cardiothoracic Center of the Korle-Bu Teaching Hospital and died on 1st September 2012.

Family

K. G. was married to the former Christina Paintsil. They were married in December 1958 and had six children: Mrs. Aba Kanyiba Wobil, who is in the hospitality industry, Mrs. Araba Kwegyirba Intsiful, an engineer, Mrs. Esi Siamba Djan, a biologist, Mrs. Aba Gyatowa Morkey, a health and wellness consultant, and Kweku Ghartey Sam, a pediatrician.

Mr. Josiah Wobil

Early Life and Education

J osiah Wobil was born in Winneba on 9th April, 1942. His parents were Kweku Kommey and Ekua Akyireh. His father was a fisherman and his mother a fish processor and trader. Neither had any formal education. Josiah has two brothers and one sister. He attended the Winneba Methodist Primary and Middle schools from 1949 through 1956. He started showing initiative and drive at an early age. As a kid, aged nine, Josiah started organizing infant masquerading groups during the Christmas season.

Between ages 10 and 14, Josiah spent the weekends hunting for crabs with friends at Woarababa village. He, along with other kids and adults, helped bring to shore, fishing canoes returning with their harvest of fish. This was his first paid job. At age twelve, Josiah applied the arithmetic lessons he had been learning in school to record accounts for the fishermen groups that supplied fish to his mother to sell. During the off-fishing seasons, Josiah also helped his parents with their shallot farming business near the Muni Lagoon, just outside Winneba. These pursuits as a kid helped Josiah develop an interest in fishing and farming which paved the way into his future career in agriculture.

Josiah gained admission to Mfantsipim Secondary School in January 1957, and completed his Ordinary-Level (O-level) examinations in June 1961 and Advanced-level (A-level) examinations in June 1963. His greatest influence and patron was his uncle, Joseph Amoako, his mother's brother, who took him under his wings and largely financed his education. Mr. Joseph Amoako was a shipping manager at the Takoradi Harbor at the time and Josiah would spend his vacations with him and his family. Josiah is profoundly grateful for the help and guidance his uncle gave him. Without that help and guidance, he would not have become the person that he is now, a highly accomplished agriculturalist. From Mfantsipim Josiah went to the University of Ghana at Legon, Accra, where he got his bachelor's degree, second class upper honors, in agriculture in 1966.

Career Path

Josiah joined the Ministry of Agriculture in 1966 after graduating from Legon, and was assigned to the Seed Multiplication Unit in the Ministry of Agriculture. His first posting was to Sunyani in the Brong Ahafo Region from 1966 through 1968 where he established a branch of the Seed Multiplication Unit. His work involved nursing high-yielding seeds and seedlings which were distributed to farmers throughout the region. In 1968, while at Sunyani, he was awarded a three-month scholarship by the United States

Agency for International Development (USAID) to attend a Summer seedsman's training program at Mississippi State University in the United States of America. That was where he learned the concept of "Seed Grower Seed Production".

On his return to Ghana, Josiah's work portfolio was expanded to include the Ashanti Region requiring his relocation to Kumasi. In 1969, he got another scholarship, this time the African-American Institute's AFGRAD Fellowship award, which sent him to the Montana State University (MSU) in Bozeman, Montana. He obtained his master's degree from MSU in seed technology in 1971. After graduation, he had a year's practical attachment with Dekalb AgResearch Inc., a major American seed company, where he was introduced to modern seed industry management.

Josiah returned to Ghana in 1972 and was posted to the head office of the Seed Multiplication Unit in Accra as Senior Agricultural Officer. He was promoted to Officer-in-Charge of the Unit in 1975. In that position, Josiah was responsible for the promotion of a national seed program that would cater to the seed needs of farms and farmers throughout the country. The Unit was principally engaged in the production, processing and storage of maize, rice, cowpea, groundnut as well as local and exotic vegetable seeds.

Josiah formed a company, the Ghana Seed Company, in 1978, and served as the company's first managing director. The company, with financial help from USAID and the German government, established a massive seed industry infrastructure of seed farms, seed processing plants, storage and marketing facilities throughout the country.

Josiah was recruited in 1988 by the United Nations Food and Agriculture Organization (FAO) as a seed technology expert. He was posted to Swaziland to manage an FAO seed project in the country. Under Josiah's guidance, the project advanced into a joint partnership between the Swazi government and the Pioneer Hi-Bred International of USA, the world's largest seed company.

From Swaziland, he was transferred to Trinidad and Tobago where he assisted in developing national seed programs not only in that country but also in Jamaica, Belize, Dominica, Antigua and Barbuda, Guyana and Surinam. In 1996, he spent some time at the FAO headquarters in Rome, where he assisted in shaping and reframing FAO policies and approaches in international seed sector assistance to member countries.

During his time at FAO headquarters, Josiah was sent on a mission to Thailand from where he led a team of experts on a tour of Asia Pacific countries to conclude FAO's 12-year seed project which had covered those countries. His consultations with the various national authorities helped formulate guidelines which led to the formation of the Asia Pacific Seed Association (APSA). APSA has progressed to become the largest regional seed association in the world and a very successful multi-billion dollar grouping that has been transforming seed industries in the Asia-Pacific region including India, China, Japan, Thailand, Australia and the Philippines.

After his stint at FAO headquarters, Josiah devoted the next several years to consultancy work in the field. He undertook several assignments relating to the provision of technical assistance to a wide range of clients including former Soviet Republics of Moldova and Uzbekistan. His consultancy work also took him to Pakistan, Libya, South Sudan, Jordan and Iraq where he assisted in establishing or restructuring their respective national seed programs. In a four-year stay in Eritrea as FAO Emergency Coordinator in the aftermath of the Eritrea-Ethiopia war, Josiah provided leadership in building, and in some cases, rebuilding key structures such as seed farms, veterinary centers, poultry farms, and organizing emergency seed production and distribution of agricultural tools to small farmers in areas that had been devastated by war.

Since retiring from FAO in 2004, Josiah has continued to serve as FAO Retiree Consultant, providing technical assistance to the

Gambia, Sierra Leone, Myanmar (Burma), Liberia and Ghana. In 2005, he was selected as the lead consultant in the formulation of the African Seed and Biotechnology Program (ASBP), a continental seed development program for the African Union. This program was formally adopted by the African heads of states and governments in Addis Ababa in 2007. Josiah has been closely involved with the implementation of that program in his capacity as Chief Advisor to the Executive Director of AfricaSeeds, the Abidjan-based institution which is closely linked with ASBP implementation.

Josiah has been involved in the formulation and adoption of a National Seed Policy and a National Seed Plan for Ghana, with assistance from FAO and USAID since 2013. He further prepared a Seed Certification and Quality Assurance Manual for Ghana, under the sponsorship of the Alliance for a Green Revolution in Africa (AGRA). Under his guidance, efforts are currently being made to enhance seed legislation and implementation in Ghana and the establishment of a Seed Sector Development Fund.

Josiah was appointed by President Nana Akuffo Addo as chairman of the National Seed Council, a national policy think tank, in 2017. The Council was charged with overseeing and coordinating all seed industry activities in the country. In 2021, he was selected by the African Union as Consultant to develop continental guidelines for the harmonization of regulatory frameworks in Africa. This was a long-awaited and strategic seed sector initiative, an assignment that is presently occupying much of his time. He has published more than 15 national seed sector policy and regulatory frameworks documents.

Entrepreneurship

Apart from all his professional accomplishments, Josiah is also an entrepreneur businessman and real estate developer. He owns a 21-room hotel named Hotel Nagy in Winneba. This hotel provides a serene and artistic ambiance for retreats, conferences and entertainment. Additionally, in response to the high demand for student accommodation for the University of Education in Winneba, he has built a three-floor, 25-room hostel for students in the town.

Family:

Josiah is married to the former Angelina Taylor and they have been blessed with four children: Anita, a banker, Perry, an electrical engineer, Terry, a chemical engineer and Nana Gyama, an accountant. His hobbies are designing clothes and landscaping.

Section B

The Academicians

Professor Joseph Yanney Ewusie

Early Life and Education

Professor Yanney Ewusie was born in Winneba on 18th April, 1927. His birth name was Joseph Yanney Wilson. His parents were Samuel Kweku Andoh Mensah Wilson and Elizabeth Ekua Akyere Dickson. His home name was Kojo Akumanyie. He attended Winneba Anglican School from 1932 – 1941. Two years after completing elementary school, his grandfather, Rev. Albert Benjamin Dickson of the Methodist Church, sent him to Mfantsipim Secondary School in Cape Coast which he successfully completed in 1947.

Yanney Ewusie continued to the University of the Gold Coast, now known as the University of Ghana, Legon, in Accra. He was one of the first batch of students admitted to the University of the

Gold Coast in 1948. He completed his bachelor's degree in botany in 1953. While at the university, he spent brief periods teaching science and biology at the Gold Coast Peoples College, later renamed Ghanatta Secondary School in Accra, Achimota School, Accra High School and Mfantsipim. He was awarded a scholarship to Cambridge University in Cambridge, England, where he earned his doctorate in 1957 at age 30. His doctoral thesis covered cyto-genetics and bluebells.

Career Path

Yanney Ewusie returned to the Gold Coast in 1957 and joined the teaching staff as lecturer in the Department of Botany at the University of Ghana. His main area of interest and research was identifying the various kinds of peppers in the Accra area. In 1963, he was appointed the first secretary general and chief executive of the Ghana Academy of Sciences by the then President Kwame Nkrumah, a position he held until 1967. Yanney Ewusie was later elected Fellow of the Academy. During his tenure, the Academy founded the Industrial Research Institute, Food Research Institute, Ghana Standards Board and Ghana Atomic Energy Commission. These institutes were established because, under the visionary guidance of Ghana's first President Kwame Nkrumah, the country needed scientific institutions that would explore and exploit the country's vast human and natural resources that would lead to the transformation not only of the country but the rest of Africa. In 1964, during the heyday of Pan Africanism, driven by the need to establish his African and Ghanaian identity, Yanney Ewusie changed his last name from Wilson to Ewusie.

Yanney Ewusie moved to the University College of Cape Coast as an assistant professor in the Department of Botany in 1969. He became head of the department later that year. In September 1970, he was appointed dean of the Faculty of Science. Concurrently, he was appointed acting vice-principal of the university in September 1971, and a full professor in January 1973.

Professional Achievements

Yanney Ewusie was appointed Vice-Chancellor of the University of Cape Coast in 1973, a position he held until 1979. In Ghana, the head of the university is the Vice-Chancellor. The chancellorship is reserved for the president of the country. It was during his tenure as vice chancellor that the following schools and departments were established: The School of Agriculture, Department of Business Studies, Department of Music, Department of Science Education and the Department of Ghana languages. He also initiated the Kwame Nkrumah Memorial Lectures and had the famous Nigerian politician and academician, Chief Obafemi Awolowo, as the inaugural guest speaker in 1976. Yanney Ewusie renamed several of the streets on the university campus to commemorate the achievements of prominent Ghanaians. Those honored included Mensah-Sarbah, Casely Hayford, and Paa Grant, to name a few.

Yanney Ewusie was elected president of the Ghana Science Association and chairman of the Scientific Committee on Problems of the Environment in 1972. In April 1978, the association organized a symposium on "Major Pollution Problems of Ghana". After the symposium a resolution was submitted to the Ghana government on the need to set up an Environmental Protection Agency or Council. The government adopted the resolution and the agency was subsequently established.

After retiring from the University of Cape Coast in 1980, Yanney Ewusie turned his attention to universities and institutions in other parts of Africa. He was a Visiting Professor at the University of Nairobi in Kenya in 1980 and taught at the Ahmadu Bello University in Zaria Kaduna State in Nigeria. He also taught at the University of Swaziland and finally at the University of Bophuthatswana in

1992. Between 1980 and 1983, he served as the first African Chief Executive of the Pan African Institute for Development (PAID) in the Republic of the Cameroons. This institute provided training, research and consultancy for personnel engaged in rural development from all over the continent. Under his leadership, work began on the construction of a branch office in Kabwe in Zambia. This center was to serve as the regional office responsible for East and Southern Africa (PAID-ESA).

Yanney Ewusie helped found PROSRAMAST in 2007. PROSRAMAST stood for Promotion for the Study, Research and Application of Mathematics, Science and Technology. This entity was a non-profit organization to promote the study of science and mathematics in junior and senior secondary schools in the country. Plans were made for a pilot program that involved quiz competitions among high school students in the Winneba-Senya Traditional area. Unfortunately the plans never got implemented.

Yanney Ewusie's passion for research is shown in an incident narrated by a friend and a colleague, Professor E. Laing, at Yanney Ewusie's funeral. Professor Laing told how Yanney Ewusie was once arrested in Accra for driving over the speed limit. When Yanney Ewusie appeared before the judge, the judge asked him why he was driving that fast. The judge told him that by law, only doctors are allowed to drive over the speed limit, and that only if life was at stake. Yanney Ewusie responded with, "Yes, indeed, life was at stake." When the judge asked him to explain, his response was, "My precious pepper plants had to be replanted very quickly before I lost them through drying and wilting." When the judge asked him what "life" was involved, Yanney Ewusie responded, "The life of the pepper seedlings!" The judge dismissed the case by admonishing him not "to bring your strange and abstruse academic arguments here!"

Professor Yaney Ewusie was a true academic. In all, he wrote four books: "Tropical Biology" 1964, which was revised in 1968 and

1974, "Tropical Biological Drawings" 1973, "Elements of Tropical Ecology" 1980 and "Phenology in Tropical Ecology" 1992. These books became classics and were used as text books from high school to university level throughout the continent. He published 46 academic articles, received nine honorary awards and was a member of 120 academic associations. Yanney Ewusie presented papers at approximately 70 conferences, seminars and workshops.

While he was visiting professor at the University of Swaziland, Yanney Ewusie instituted the Swaziland Journal of Science and Technology and served as the journal's first editor for two years. As a visiting professor at the University of Bophuthatswana, he founded the Bophuthatswana Association for Scientific Advancement, and served as its first president for the first three years. Yanney Ewusie was honored by the Ghana Science Association as the "Scientist of the Year" in 1982. The University of Cape Coast honored him with a Doctor of Science (D.Sc.) degree in 1994. He was Fellow of the Linnaean Society, a member of the World Academy of Arts and Science, and a member of the Board of International Council for Scientific Unions from 1964 through 1967.

Family Life

Yanney Ewusie was very friendly. He enjoyed dancing, travelling and stimulating conversation. In his mid-twenties, he taught ball-room dancing in Winneba. He had a wry sense of humor. His son, Kwamina Owen Ewusie, tells one of his father's favorite jokes. A man meets a friend he hadn't seen in years and asks him how his wife, Audrey, was doing. The friend responded, "Audrey is in Heaven." The man naturally responded with, "I am very sorry to hear that." The friend asked, "Are you sad that my wife is in heaven?" The man bashfully replied, "No, No, No, I am glad that she is in heaven." The friend replied, "So are you happy that my wife is dead?"

Yanney Ewusie was a lifelong member of the Winneba Ebenezer Methodist Church. He attended Bible Study classes and was always willing to help raise funds for the church. Anytime he was in Accra, he attended the Legon Interdenominational Church on the university campus.

Yanney Ewusie was patriarch of the extended family and helped form the Na Yɛ Na Descendants Association, named after his great grandmother in 1993. He lost his first wife, Stella Turkson, in 1989 after thirty years of marriage and five children. He married his second wife, Ruth Parry, affectionately called Mama Ruth, in 1998. Mama Ruth was a loving, caring wife who took great care of him in his evening years until his passing. Yanney Ewusie died on 14th June 2012, at age 85.

Most Rev. Professor Kwesi Abotsia Dickson

Early Life and Education

Kwesi Abotsia Dickson was born in Saltpond on 7th July, 1929. His parents were the Rev. Albert Benjamin Charles Doku Dickson from Winneba and Victoria Tabitha Esi Aakowa Atta Dadson from Gomoa Adzentam'. He was the second of four siblings and the first of three boys. He attended Methodist Primary Schools in Winneba and Cape Coast from 1939 to 1943. Kwesi Dickson went to Mfantsipim Secondary School in 1943 and completed form five, passing the Cambridge School Certificate examination with Grade 1, with exemption from London Matriculation.

Kwesi Dickson continued to Trinity College in Kumasi in 1951. He transferred to the University of the Gold Coast now University of Ghana, Legon, in 1952. He graduated in 1956 with a bachelor's degree in divinity, first-class. He proceeded to Mansfield College, Oxford University, where he obtained his bachelor of letters degree in 1959, specializing in Old Testament Rituals and Divine Forgiveness. He spent 1959 at the University of Chicago as a Ford Foundation Exchange Fellow.

Career Path

Kwesi Dickson, as he was called by all who knew him, began his academic career as a tutor in the Department for the Study of Religions at the University of Ghana in 1961. The university recognized his exceptional scholarship as he rose to lecturer, senior lecturer, associate professor, culminating in his promotion to a full professor at the university in 1969. He served as the head of department on more than one occasion. From 1980 through 1987, he was director of the Institute of African Studies.

Kwesi Dickson was the Henry Luce Visiting professor of World Christianity at the Union Theological Seminary in New York. He was also Visiting Professor at the University of Swaziland, an external examiner in West Africa and Eastern African universities and the Akrofi-Christaller Center for Mission Research and Applied Theology at Akropong-Akwapim. He was a fellow of the Ghana Academy of Arts and Sciences and served two consecutive terms as president. Kwesi Dickson retired as Professor Emeritus after being inducted into that esteemed position in 1993. He authored about a dozen books and several academic articles.

Life in the Church

Kwesi Dickson started his Christian ministry in August 1954, at age 25, when he served as a probationary minister in the Sekondi District of the Gold Coast Methodist Church. He was ordained as a Methodist minister at the British Conference meeting in Nottingham in 1957, while he was a student at Oxford University. Back in Ghana, in October 1960, he served as circuit minister at Elmina. At the University of Ghana, Legon, during the 1960s, he served as the pastor for the Methodist congregation in Legon Hall for their Sunday morning worship services. Decades later when the Interdenominational Church was built on the Legon campus, he served as the pastor from 1980 through 1988. In 1990, he was inducted as the seventh president of the Methodist Conference and served until 1997.

Kwesi Dickson held several positions in the Church. On the national and world stages, Kwesi Dickson served on the Faith and Order Committee of the World Council of Churches and was first chairman of the West African Association of Theological Institutions. He was also president of the Ghana Theological Association, a member of the World Methodist Executive Council, vice-president and finally president of the All Africa Conference of Churches (AACC). He was president of AACC from 1997 until 2003. He also served as chairperson of the committee that drew up the new liturgy for the Ghana Methodist Church. He was instrumental in founding the Dunwell Insurance Company. This company helped establish an Endowment Fund which funded the Methodist University College in Accra.

Kwesi Dickson delivered the tenth address in the J. B. Danquah Memorial Lectures Series in February 1977. He also delivered the 170th anniversary lectures of the Methodist Church, Ghana, at the Calvary Methodist Church in Accra in August 2005. He died two months later that year at age 76.

Family Life

Kwesi Dickson's hobbies were tennis and organ playing. At the time of his death in October 2005, he was survived by his wife, the former Cecilia Elizabeth Mensah, whom he married in 1961, and four children, Kwesi, Kodwo, Efua and Kofi. He was celebrated by many groups including the Mfantsipim Old Boys Association MOBA '48. This group was unique to the school because it produced a cabinet minister, a Supreme Court judge, top civil servants, university professors, ambassadors to several foreign countries, presidents and vice president of the Ghana Methodist Conference and church.

Other groups that celebrated Kwesi Dickson's achievements were the Ghana Academy of Arts and Sciences, the Fellowship of Christian Councils and Churches in West Africa, All AFRICA Conference of Churches, the Ghana Methodist Church Holland Mission Circuit, World Council of Churches, World Methodist Council, London Wesley Chapel, World Alliance of Reformed Churches, the Christian Council of Ghana and the University of Ghana, Legon.

Mr. Christopher John Yarney

Early Life and Education

Christopher was born at Penkye in Winneba on 23rd September, 1929. He was the third child of Christopher John Yarney, Snr. and the former Mercy Sackey also of Penkye. Christopher started his schooling at the Government Boys' School in Cape Coast where he was living with his uncle, Sam M. H. B. Yarney, musician, also profiled in this book. He moved to live with his parents in Kumasi where he continued his primary education at Basel School. His third move as a young boy was to Accra where he attended the Methodist Boys' School. He had his secondary education at Adisadel College in Cape Coast, excelling in his final year, 1949, winning prizes in English and Classics. He taught briefly at the Government Boys' School in Yendi, in Northern Ghana, before going to the University of Ghana, Legon, for his bachelor's degree in English and Classics.

Career Path

Christopher joined the Ministry of Education after graduation from the University of Ghana, Legon, and was posted to Cape Coast as Senior Education Officer. After a few years, he left to teach English at Takoradi Technical Institute, now Takoradi Technical University. He was later appointed vice-principal at Peki Government Training College. He and five other Ghanaian officers at the Ministry of Education were sent to Zanzibar to help the country restructure its educational system. They were in Zanzibar for five years.

On his return to Ghana, Christopher was assigned to the Ministry of Education as the chief courses officer and head of the Inspectorate Division. He hosted the Ghana Broadcasting Corporation program, "Talking Point", for a while in Accra. He was appointed principal of the Advanced Teacher Training College (ATTC) in Winneba in 1970. The campus of the college had initially been built for the former Kwame Nkrumah Ideological Institute. The institute was shut down after the coup d'etat that overthrew the government of Kwame Nkrumah in February 1966. Christopher served in that capacity for nine years.

One of the major projects Christopher undertook at the Institute was a modern sewage disposal system that relied on aerated ponds. This improved the sanitary conditions at the University campus considerably. During his tenure as principal, the following buildings were constructed: Ghartey Hall Annex, the Osagyefo Library, the departments of Science Education, French and English. He also oversaw the construction of apartments for lecturers. He established the Demonstration School and later the Experimental Junior Secondary School where the teacher trainees could obtain practical training as part of their education. The ATTC is now the South Campus of the University of Education, Winneba. The Demonstration School is now University Primary and Junior Secondary School.

Christopher took a year off during the 1971/72 academic year to get his master's degree in philosophical foundations of education and educational psychology at the University of South Florida. Part of his training in the United States, which was sponsored by the United States Agency for International Development (USAID), was in the area of Teacher Education Administration. This involved organizing teacher training on multiple campuses. This was later on to form the basis of the three campuses of the University of Education, Winneba. He returned to his position as principal of the college in 1972. He was forced to quit in 1979 due to student demonstrations against conditions at the college. He retired from the Ghana Education Service, as the Ministry of Education was known then, in 1981. He got a job as lecturer at the University College of Education at Gumel in Kano State, Nigeria. He returned to Ghana in 1989 and settled in Winneba.

Achievements

During Christopher's tenure as principal, the college became a major source of employment for Winneba. He revived all the construction projects on campus that had been abandoned following the overthrow of Kwame Nkrumah and the closing down of the Ideological Institute. Those projects, along with the carpentry and fitting workshops established on the campus, provided jobs for the town's many unemployed.

Christopher was instrumental in the founding of the Nurses Training College in Winneba. He helped provide temporary accommodation for the new staff and students prior to the construction of permanent buildings and structures on the school grounds. He also reorganized the College Farm which produced poultry, beef and vegetables, and a fishing venture with the local fishermen to reduce student feeding costs. This farm was recognized by the then Chairman of the National Redemption Council, General Ignatius Kutu Akyeampong, as one of the best in the country. The farm's recognition was important because it provided a spotlight that showcased the military government's campaign of "Operation Feed Yourself". After his stint as director of the ATTC, Christopher was appointed the Secretary to the National Committee on Universal Primary education Program. The Committee's recommendations led to the establishment of the Junior Secondary School System that is still in force throughout the country.

Family Life

Christopher was a Christian and a Bible scholar. He knew Greek and had a copy of the original Bible in the Greek language. He was married to the former Virginia Dora Amuasi. He died on 24th May, 2007 at age 78, leaving behind his wife, Dora, nine children, several nephews and nieces.

Professor Daniel Kwamina Abbiw Jackson

Early Life and Education

A bbiw Jackson, as he was known throughout his life, was born in Winneba on Saturday, 27th September, 1930. He was the first born of six children of the late Mr. Daniel Kwesi Abbiw Jackson of the Royal Family of Senya Beraku and the late Madam Joana Aba Yamoah of Winneba. Both parents were talented in school. The father started work as a bookkeeper and accounts clerk, of remarkable brilliance and promise with F. and A. Swanzy, a trading company at Winneba which later became part of the United Africa Company (U.A.C.). The mother was a business woman who operated a clothing business with merchandise bought from the U.A.C.

Abbiw's younger siblings, Joseph, Osborne and Ebenezer are also featured in this book.

Soon after the birth of Abbiw Jackson, the family moved to Saltpond where he started his primary school education in 1936 and continued at Cape Coast in 1940 where the father had been transferred. In December 1944, Abbiw-Jackson's exceptional abilities became public when he passed the Standard Seven Certificate Examination with distinction, and gained admission into Mfantsipim, Adisadel and Achimota Secondary School, the three famous senior high schools in the country then. Observing how brilliant Abbiw Jackson was, judging from his scores, the headmasters of these schools competed among themselves appealing to Abbiw and the parents for Abbiw to select their school. Mr. Francis Lodowick Bartels, then Acting Headmaster of Mfantsipim, succeeded in winning Abbiw over to Mfantsipim, where Abbiw was destined to set the standard for all future mathematicians in Ghana and perhaps in Africa.

Abbiw attended Mfantsipim Secondary School from 1945 to 1949. His spectacular academic achievements at Mfantsipim are almost legendary. He was an outstanding student from start to finish, never going below the first position in class with relative ease and without toiling all night studying. His desire to excel in almost every subject endeared him to all who taught him. In his final high school year certificate Examinations in 1950, he obtained seven As including English Language in the eight subjects he took in the examination. He was short of one mark from the grade of A in Fante. He was awarded the enviable prize of the "Best Scholar of the Year".

Abbiw continued to the University College of the Gold Coast in Accra in 1950, where he studied for the Intermediate B.Sc. in physics, chemistry, pure and applied mathematics and honors in mathematics as an external student of London University. Abbiw was considered a genius in mathematics and vied for the first position in class at the University College with another bril-liant student from Achimota Secondary School. This high level of scholarship by the two students somehow became a competition between their two high schools, Achimota and Mfantsipim.

It was reported at the time, that when the final Intermediate B.Sc. examination results were released, the Achimotan scored two marks short of 100%. He immediately started to celebrate victory along with his school mates. It was during this merry-making and shoulder-patting that the surprising news flashed that Abbiw had scored 116%! This was incredible. Incidentally, at that time, one could obtain full marks by answering a specified number of ques-tions in the given time, which the Achimotan did. However, one could also answer more or all the other optional questions which Abbiw-Jackson did. With this singular performance, Abbiw established his fame and excellence in mathematics at the University College.

Abbiw pursued his education in mathematics to obtain his B.Sc. (Special), First-Class in mathematics as an external student of the University of London, in 1955. He was the first Ghanaian to obtain the First-Class degree in the University College of the Gold Coast. This unprecedented incredible achievement and record made Abbiw a much sought-after darling of everybody. He continued his academic studies at Trinity College, Cambridge University, where he passed the Mathematics-Tripos Part II in 1956, and Mathematics-Tripos Part III in 1957.

Career Path

On his return to Ghana after his master's degree, Abbiw took up an appointment as a tutor at Mfantsipim, his alma mater, for two years, before joining the Mathematics Department at the University of Science and Technology (UST) in Kumasi in 1959 as a lecturer. While at the university, he was granted study leave to

Imperial College, University of London, where he obtained the Doctor of Philosophy degree in algebra in 1965.

Abbiw participated in several courses abroad. He was an Alexander von Humboldt Postgraduate Fellow at the University of Frankfurt during the 1965/66 academic year. He was also a visiting Associate Professor and a Fulbright-Hayes Scholar at the Massachusetts Institute of Technology (MIT) in 1976/77.

Abbiw was interested in mathematics education and devoted his entire life to that cause. From 1962 to 1969, under the sponsorship of the Educational Development Centre of Newton in Massachusetts, USA, Abbiw participated in the annual Summer Writing Workshops held in Entebbe, Uganda and Mombasa, Kenya. These workshops produced the Entebbe Series of mathematics text-books which were later, from 1971 to 1974, adapted for use in primary, middle, secondary schools and training colleges in Ghana, Sierra Leone and Liberia. During the same period he was the co-chairman of the Secondary Writing Group which produced an excellent text on additional mathematics at the Ordinary-Level (O-Level) and advanced mathematics at Advanced-Level (A-Level).

Abbiw was the chief examiner in mathematics for the West Africa Examinations Council for several years, and the moving spirit behind the Mathematics Association of Ghana. He was the association's president from 1980 to 1985. He was an external examiner for the bachelor's degree examinations in mathematics for the University of Cape Coast, University of Ghana, and the University of Botswana, Gaborone. Abbiw contributed immensely to the work of statutory and ad-hoc committees of the Kwame Nkrumah University of Science and Technology, (KNUST), Kumasi, both academic and non- academic, and very often acted as the head of department in the absence of the substantive head. In 1987, Abbiw left KNUST to join the Inter-African Electrical Engineering College in Bingerville, Cote d'Ívoire to continue his academic career.

Family Life

With all his achievements, Abbiw remained a friendly and an unassuming colleague and friend. He was very polite and pleasant. As the first born child of his parents, who, having lost his father early and without an alternative, Abbiw had to assume premature responsibility of supporting and sustaining his three younger brothers and two sisters. He did this well and was able to hold the siblings together.

While a doctoral candidate in Britain in 1963, Abbiw married the former Cynthia Bamford, a daughter of Ghana's first Inspector-General of Police. Cynthia was a source of joy and support to Abbiw until he passed on to eternity on 9th March 1990. Abbiw left behind a wife and five children, a male and four females, with unique educational achievements. Four out of the five children pursued mathematics-related fields in the University, namely, engineering, computer science and mathematics. One of the females obtained a First-Class and a Ph.D. in mathematics and another one is a medical officer.

Mr. Joseph Samuel Gyakye Jackson

Early Life and Education

Joseph was born in Winneba on 14th April, 1933. His parents were Mr. Daniel Kwesi Abbiw Jackson of Senya Beraku and Madam Joana Aba Yamoah of Winneba. He attended Methodist primary and middle schools in Saltpond, Cape Coast, Sekondi, Tarkwa and Elmina. He went to Achimota in 1946 passing in 1952 with Grade 1 in the Cambridge School Certificate Examination with seven A's out of eight subjects. He passed the Higher School Certificate examination with distinction in all four subjects; mathematics, Further mathematics, physics and chemistry.

Joseph was admitted to the University College of the Gold Coast in 1953 where he studied mathematics as an external student of London University. He obtained a first-class honors degree in mathematics in 1956. He continued on to Trinity College at

Cambridge University where he passed the Mathematics Tripos Part II in 1958 and Mathematics Tripos Part III in 1959.

Career Path

Joseph started his career in 1962 as lecturer in the Department of Mathematics at the University of Ghana, Legon. He retired in 1984 as senior lecturer. He participated in the annual Summer Writing Workshop held in Entebbe in Uganda (1962) and Mombasa in Kenya (1966 and 1968). These workshops resulted in the Modern Mathematics workbooks that became standard text books for elementary and middle schools and training colleges.

Career Achievements

Joseph was chief examiner for the West African Examinations Council for mathematics and Additional mathematics for Ordinary Level and chief examiner for mathematics for Advanced Level between 1963 and 1983. He published articles in the Ghana Journal of Science Vol. 1, 1971 and the Journal of Geophysical Research in 1971 and 1976. He was editor for Modern Mathematics Books 1, 2 and 3, Teacher Guides 1, 2 and 3. These were published in 1987, 1988 and 1993. He was also editor for Mathematical Methods for Mathematics, Science and Engineering Students, Volume 1, 2002.

Professional Associations

Joseph was a member of the Mathematical Association of Ghana as well as the Ghana Science Association (GSA) for a number of years. He held the position of treasurer for GSA for some years.

Family and Hobbies

Joseph and his wife, Alfredtina, have four daughters. The eldest has a first-class in chemistry from Imperial College in London. Another has a first-class in Fine Art from the Kwame Nkrumah University of Science and Technology (KNUST). The other two studied electrical engineering and architecture at KNUST.

Joseph has been involved in Christian activities since his university student years and has been worshipping at Trinity College at Legon. Joe was a hockey goalkeeper and played for Akuafo Hall and the university while a student at the University of Ghana, Legon. He also played for Trinity College at Cambridge University in England. He currently watches hockey games on television.

Professor George Kwamena Tetteh

Early Years and Education:

George was born in Senya Beraku on 29th May, 1937. His parents were Mr. Isaac B. Tetteh and the former Ms. Grace Chintoh. His father, Isaac, was a businessman who traveled to several African countries to buy food products for sale in Ghana. George started his elementary education at the Senya Beraku Native Authority School and later the Local Council School in 1942 and finished in 1951. He won a scholarship to Mfantsipim Secondary School in 1952 and passed his General Certificate of Education Ordinary Level examination in 1955 and the Advanced Level examination in 1957.

George taught mathematics and general science at Mfantsipim from January to August in 1958 before proceeding to the University College of Ghana in October of the same year. Those days, the pre-university school year followed the calendar year from January through December. The university year was different, beginning in October and ending in June. So students finishing their high school in December had to wait until the following October to enter the university. George graduated from the University of Ghana, Legon, in 1961, with a Second Class Upper Division honors degree in physics. He was awarded a scholarship to the University of Saskatchewan, Canada, where he obtained his master's degree in radiation physics in 1963 and doctorate in 1967.

Career Path

George returned to Ghana in 1967 and joined the staff at the University of Ghana as a lecturer in the Department of Physics. He taught a number of undergraduate courses until 1974 when he transferred to the Ghana Atomic Energy Commission as Senior Scientific Officer. He was promoted to Principal Scientific Officer in 1976. He later transferred to the National Nuclear Research Center (NNRC) as head of the Physics Department. He was promoted to the directorship position in 1980. As director of the NNRC, he was in charge of the following departments: Physics and Electronics, Chemistry, Biology, Food and Agriculture, Reactor technology and Nuclear Medicine. He was also responsible for the International Atomic Energy's technical assistance and fellowship programs.

George returned to the University of Ghana as associate professor and head of the Department of Physics in October 1983, a position he held until October 1991. He was promoted to a professorship position in December 1993.

George's research interests have been in nuclear and radiation technology. He has participated in many International Atomic

Energy Agency programs in X-Ray Fluorescence science. He has published over 50 articles in refereed journals and participated in many workshops, symposia, seminars and colloquia. He has also attended many international conferences.

George was Vice-President of the Ghana Institute of Physics, a member of the International Radiation Physics Society, the Ghana Science Association and a Fellow of the Ghana Academy of Arts and Sciences. He has also served as a member of two boards: the Ghana Atomic Energy Commission, and the Council for Scientific and Industrial Research (CSIR). He has supervised several master's and doctoral degree candidates at the Physics Department at the University and has been an external examiner on several occasions to the University of Cape Coast and the West African Examinations Council since 1971.

Family Life

Professor Tetteh was married to the former Elizabeth Love Osei, an elementary school teacher. They have five children, three girls and two boys. One of the girls is a medical doctor and the other two are in nursing leadership and administrative positions. Both boys work as systems administrators for various organizations.

George was a member of the Mfantsipim Old Boys Association. He practiced Hinduism and worshipped at the Hindu Monastery of Africa located at Odorkor in Accra. He served as the president of the Ghana branch of the Divine Life Society for several years. He loved to play soccer as a young man and in his later years loved to watch games on television. He was an avid boxing fan and loved dancing. He died in May 2014.

Professor Osborne Augustus Yamoah Jackson

Early Life and Education

Osborne is the fourth of six children and the third of four boys. He was born on 7th July, 1938 in Saltpond. His father, Daniel Kwesi Abbiw Jackson, was from Senya Beraku and his mother, Joana Emma Yamoah, was from Winneba. Osborne started his elementary education in Cape Coast in 1944. The family moved to Winneba that same year. Osborne was eleven years old when his father died. That was a traumatic experience for him. He was sent to stay with an uncle, Eduonum Jackson, also in Winneba. He sat for the Common Entrance Examination in 1952. Osborne did so well in the examination and the subsequent interview that out of more than 100 students who were selected to go to Achimota Secondary School in January 1953, he was one of three students who were placed in form two, thus skipping form one.

Osborne got seven As (excellent) out of eight subjects and one B in the Form Five School Certificate Examination held in 1956. He did his sixth form also at Achimota which he completed in 1958. He passed the Higher School Certificate Examination with As in mathematics, further mathematics and chemistry and B in physics. This performance earned him "Cambridge Scholar" when he was admitted to the University of Ghana, Legon, in October 1959. He obtained a bachelor of science degree in mathematics at Legon in 1962.

Osborne did his master's degree in statistics at Birmingham University in Midlands in the United Kingdom between 1962 and 1963. He continued to Birkbeck College, London University, then transferred to Imperial College where he completed his doctorate in statistics. In his final year as a doctoral candidate in August 1966, Osborne taught statistics to final year students at the then Kingston College of Technology.

Career Path

On returning to Ghana in 1966, Osborne taught statistics at the Kwame Nkrumah University of Science and Technology in Kumasi for three years. He left the university to work for the Bank of Ghana in 1972. In 1980, he was selected, among five competing candidates, to become Government Statistician, making him head of the Central Bureau of Statistics. The Bureau was then preparing to undertake the 1980 national census. The census was delayed by the December 31, 1981 coup d'etat led by Flight Lieutenant Jerry John Rawlings.

The early months of the coup were quite harrowing. The military administration harassed the senior personnel in the government departments although the government still depended on them for their expertise in administering the country. Osborne cites one instance that still sends shivers down his spine. He and his colleague, Dr. Alhassan Mohamed of the Bank of Ghana, were summoned by Jerry Rawlings, chairman of the Provisional National Defense Council (PNDC), to Gondar Barracks at Burma Camp. Earlier, senior civil servants who had been summoned to the barracks for consultation had had their heads shaved by the soldiers at the barracks! When he and Dr. Mohamed got to the barracks, they were ordered out of their vehicles and asked to put their hands on their heads with guns pointed at them! They were marched into the offices of Jerry Rawlings, where they met with Rawlings and his team. At one of those meetings, there was a blackout and everybody panicked. When the lights came back on a few minutes later, Rawlings was holding a machine gun at the ready!

Osborne was transferred back to the Bank of Ghana in January 1982, this time, as the Second Deputy Governor. In December 1983, with the Ghanaian economy in tatters and food scarce everywhere in the country, Osborne left the Bank of Ghana to work with the International Civil Service Commission at the United Nations in New York. He worked at the United Nations from 1984 through 1999. Osborne retired from the United Nations Statistics Division in March 1999.

He did consulting work with the Committee on Development Information for the Economic Commission for Africa (ECA) in June 1999 and the International Maritime Organization in 2000. He moved back to Ghana in 2002 where he has been teaching statistics at the Methodist University College in Accra. Osborne was awarded Best Teacher at the university college in 2008.

Osborne has presented papers on statistics at various conferences and workshops in and outside the country. He has served on the Council of the Institute of Professional Studies in Accra since 2009.

Family Life

Osborne has been a Methodist all his life. Since his return to Ghana, he has been a member of the Mount Olivet Methodist Church in Dansoman in Accra, and serves on the Methodist University Governing Council. Osborne and his wife, Millicent, have been blessed with three children, Osborne Jnr., Audrey and Derek.

Professor Daniel Afedzi Akyeampong

Early Life and Education

Daniel was born in Senya Beraku on 24th November, 1938. He was the last born of Peter Napoleon Akyeampong and Ms. Charity Afful, both from Senya Beraku. Daniel attended Senya Beraku Local Council School from 1945 to 1953. He gained admission to Mfantsipim Secondary School in 1954, joining the class of Form 2 instead of the regular Form 1 because of his high scores in the Common Entrance Examination. In his final year at Mfantsipim in 1959, he won the "Best Student in Physical Sciences and Mathematics" award. He entered the University of Ghana in 1960 and graduated in 1963 with a bachelor of science degree in mathematics. He won scholarships to the University of London and Imperial College in London and attended classes in both institutions. He obtained his doctorate in mathematical physics in October 1966 from the University of London and a diploma in mathematical physics from Imperial College in November that same year.

Career Path

Daniel returned to Ghana in 1966 and joined the staff of the Department of Mathematics at the University of Ghana as a lecturer. He held many positions at the university, ranging from senior lecturer in 1972 to associate professor in 1976. He became the first Ghanaian to attain a full professorship in mathematics in 1982. He was twice head of the Department of Mathematics from 1976 to 1983, and from 1985 to 1988. He was the Pro-Vice Chancellor of the university from 1988 through 1992. As Pro-Vice Chancellor, he was the chairman of the Academic Planning Committee, the Estimates Committee, the Housing Committee, the Management Committee of the Housing Loan Scheme, the Residence Board, and the advisory boards of all the institutes in the university. He also served on several other committees including the Inter-Faculty Committee on Regulations Governing the bachelor's degree at the university.

Daniel was a visiting lecturer at several universities during his career. He was a Commonwealth Academic Staff Fellow and Visiting Senior Lecturer at the Imperial College of Science and Technology in London, a Visiting Scientist at the International Center for Theoretical Physics in Triese, Italy, a Visiting Professor at the University of Cape Coast, and a Visiting Professor at the University of Science and Technology in Port Harcourt in Nigeria. At one point, he was the head of the Department of Mathematics and dean of the Faculty of Science at the University of Science and Technology in Port Harcourt.

Daniel was honored to have had the late Professor Abdus Salam, the 1979 Nobel Laureate in physics, as his supervisor and mentor. In 1964, under the leadership of Professor Salam, the International Center for Theoretical Physics, Trieste, Italy, was established to promote the study of physics and mathematical sciences in developing countries. Daniel was one of the first fellows of the Center in 1964/65, an associate from 1967 to 1975, a senior associate from 1976 to 1993, and an honorary associate in 1994. In October 2014 he was honored as a "Pioneer Fellow" at the 50th anniversary of the Center.

Professional Achievements

During his tenure as professor at the universities listed above, George was also a member of the following institutions in Ghana: National Council for Higher Education (1972 – 1980), the Council for Scientific and Industrial Research (1975 – 1978 and 1992 – 1997), and the National Implementation Committee on Tertiary Education Reforms (1989 – 1992). He was the Honorary Secretary of the Ghana Academy of Arts and Sciences (1975 – 1978). He also served as a representative of the University of Ghana on the Ghana National Committee of the West African Examinations Council (1992 – 1996), and a member of the National Council for Tertiary Education (1993 – 2004).

Daniel was also chairman of the National Accreditation Board (1994 – 2004), president of the Mathematical Association of Ghana (1988 – 1994), and vice-president of the Ghana Academy of Arts and Sciences (1995 – 1998). He was chairman of the Committee on Evaluation of National Policy Objectives on Tertiary Education, Ministry of Education (1988), and chairman of the Committee to Review the Grading System for the Basic Education Certificate Examination (BECE) 1999.

In addition to all of those responsibilities, he was chairman of the Country Selection Committee for the Ford Foundation International Fellowship Program (2000 – 2002), chairman of the West African Examinations Council Committee on the Leakage of the BECE (2002), a member of the President's Committee of the Review of Education Reforms in Ghana (2002), and a member of the Board of Trustees of the Ghana Education Trust Fund (2003 – 2005).

On the international arena, Daniel was the assistant editor of Africa Matematica, a journal of the African Mathematical Union. He was also a member of the Editorial Advisory Board for Discovery and Innovation, a journal of the African Academy of Sciences, a reviewer for Mathematical Review in Michigan, USA (1976 – 1994), and a member of the Advisory Board on World Science Report, United Nations Education and Scientific Organization (UNESCO), Paris, in 1988. He was a member of the Standing Committee on Freedom in the Conduct of Science of the International Council for Science (1986 – 1993), a member of the Executive Board of the International Council for Science, Paris, in 1993, and also served as the Council's vice-president from 1996 through 1999.

Daniel wrote one book, "The Two Cultures Revisited: Interactions of Science and Culture". This was a compilation of a series of lectures he delivered at the 25th J. B. Danquah Memorial Lectures, and was published by the Ghana Academy of Arts and Sciences. He published about 26 articles in peer-reviewed journals, and attended over 100 international conferences and workshops on mathematics and science where he served as chairman, panelist or moderator.

Community Involvement

Daniel was instrumental in establishing the Methodist University in Ghana, and served as a member of the university's

Advisory Board in 1996. He also served as a member of the Tertiary Education Advisory Council of the university. He was a member of the Board of Education and Youth for the Methodist Church of Ghana, chairman of the Committee on Education and Youth for the Calvary Methodist Society in Accra, and chairman of the Board of Governors for Senya Senior Secondary School.

Daniel was an active member of the Calvary Methodist Church in Adabraka, where he worshiped regularly for over 50 years. He was a member of the Men's Fellowship, the Monday Bible Class and a patron of the Church's Singing Band.

Family Life

Daniel was married to Ms. Charlotte Sally Newton, and the couple was blessed with three children, Angelo Ekow, Adrian Kofi and Adelaide Akooley. At his death on 7th March 2015 at the age of 76, he was survived by his wife of 45 years, the three children, nine grandchildren and a host of nephews and nieces.

Professor Henry Walter Richardson

Early Years and Education

Henry was born on 15th November, 1941. Both parents came from Winneba. He attended Achimota Secondary School in Accra in 1955 and by 1961, had obtained his General Certificate of Education, Ordinary and Advanced Level certificates. He continued to Philips Academy in Andover, Massachusetts in 1962 for his bachelor's degree. He then went to Cornell University, Ithaca, New York, where he obtained his B.Arch. degree in 1968, M.Arch. degree in 1970 and M.R.P. degree in 1971.

Career Path

Henry started his professional career as an architectural designer with James Cubitt and Partners, an architectural, engineering and planning company in London, England, in 1968. In 1969, he worked as a housing and urban design consultant for the Housing Agency in the Commonwealth of Puerto Rico in San Juan Puerto Rico.

Henry joined the faculty at the Department of Architecture in the College of Architecture, Art and Planning at Cornell University, Ithaca in New York in 1969, as an instructor. In 1971, he was promoted to assistant professor. He was promoted to associate professor with tenure in 1977 and full professor in 1995. Henry was interim chairman of the department from 1978 to 1980, assistant dean of the College from 1977 to 1985, acting dean from 1994 to 1997, Faculty-in-Residence for the Court-Kay-Bauer Hall at the university from 2001 to 2007, and director of the M. Arch. Program from 2008 to 2010.

Henry was a visiting associate professor of architecture and city planning at Howard University, Washington DC from 1977 to 1978, an architectural critic at the Department of Architecture at the University of Lagos, Nigeria, in 1981, a visiting associate professor and workshop coordinator at the University of Mexico, Mexico City in 1985. He was also a visiting critic at the Department of Architecture at Kuwait University in Safat, Kuwait, in 2000 and 2007, and a visiting professor of architecture and planning at the College of Environmental Design at King Fahd University in Saudi Arabia, from 1998 – 2000.

Henry served as visiting critic at the Faculty of Architecture and Planning at the Kwame Nkrumah University of Science and Technology, Kumasi, Ghana in 1976 and 2014. Henry has served on graduate seminars and design juries in several schools of architecture in both the United States and overseas. In 2014, he was the leader of Cornell's Student Multidisciplinary Applied Research Team (SMART) to Ghana to help develop a plan for micro-financing for housing.

Henry was technical advisor and leader of two missions to Ghana on Affordable Housing in 1974 and 1976. Henry was project director and principal investigator of a National Research Program on Solar Cities and Renewable Energy in the Built Environment for the United States Department of Energy and the American Institute of Architecture Research Foundation from 1978 to 1981. He was also principal investigator and co-organizer of an international symposium on Creativity in the Arts and Sciences at Cornell University in 1995.

Henry is a registered architect in the state of New York, a certified city and regional planner, USA, a charter member of the American Institute of Certified Planners, a charter member of American Planning Association and member of the International Association of Housing Science. He is the founder and principal of Concepta International, an architectural and urban design consultancy, and also the founder and principal of Henry Richardson Associates, an architectural interiors and urban design firm.

Professional Achievements

Henry has been outstanding with respect to pedagogical innovations. He was a co-developer or co-sponsor of five college-level courses. He has also individually developed, designed, and taught several courses and programs. These include a Graduate Urban Design Studio for both planning and architecture students (1971 – 1973), the first Urban Design Studio in the department's undergraduate design curriculum (1973 – 1976), the first P.C.–based Computer Graphics Studio (1990), and the first CAVE-based Intelligent Design Studio in the College of Environmental Design at King Fahd University of Petroleum and Minerals in Dhahran, Saudi Arabia (1999 – 2001).

Other college-level programs Henry designed and taught are a Collaboratory Extension to the Cornell CAVE in the Theory Center (2001 – 2010), the first CAVE-based Immersive Virtual Reality Design Studio (2001 – 2010), a joint studio with Roma Tre in the university's Rome Program (Spring 2016), and the Virtual Places XR Design Research Studio (2019 – present).

While at the Kuwait University's Department of Architecture in 2007, Henry won the first-of-its kind United States National Architectural Accrediting Board accreditation outside the United States for the department. He also helped develop an educational plan and instructional program for graduate studies in architecture for the university.

Henry has written several books, monographs, articles and reports. He has presented papers at several conferences, symposia, seminars and workshops. He was co-chair of the Green Urbanism Conference in Rome, Italy in October 2006. This conference was sponsored by the International Experts for Research Enrichment and Knowledge Exchange. He was also a member of the Review and Editorial Board for IEREK-Springer Scientific Publications, and Urban Planning and Architectural Design for Sustainable Development from 2014 to 2016.

Major Projects

Henry has designed several major projects. Among these are: Visitors' Center and New Women's Hall of Fame for Seneca Falls in New York, Architectural Studies for New Town for Nasco Industries in Lagos, Nigeria, (2001 - 2003), and the Central Accra Redevelopment Plan (2004 to present). He also developed the Master Plan for Developing Umnini Trust Lands in Kwazulu Natal province in the Republic of South Africa (1998 to 2000), a Casino

Hotel and tourist resort in Durban, South Africa, a Master Plan and Urban Design for Federal Capital City, Abuja, in 1980, Vision 2000 for Brown's Race Historic District Redevelopment Master Plan (1993), and Pedestrian and Bicycle Network for Radisson New Town in Radisson in New York, (1993 – 1994).

Other major projects Henry designed include the Civic Plaza Rehabilitation Plan for Binghamton in New York, the housing estate for executive staff as well as the Ibo Iboku New Town in the Cross River state in Nigeria (1982), the Urban Design for Rochester in New York (1989 and 1993), and Planning and Urban Design for the Center of Groton in New York (1994). He also designed the Phase 2 Architectural Design of Ithaca Science Center in New York in 1993, a Research Campus for the Nigerian National Petroleum Corporation, the Brick Housing Demonstration Project in Ghana, and the Palm Court Hotel and Business Center in Accra, Ghana.

Committees and Professional Associations

Henry has served on several committees in the Department of Architecture and the wider Cornell University. He served three times as chair of the Petitions Committee between 2011 and 2020, and was chair of promotions and tenure committees from 1978 to 2007. He has been a member of the following committees: Mentoring since 1980, Admissions since 1974, Career Explorations from 1975 - 2019, M. Arch. Curriculum, Coordinating and Admissions from 2008 - 2011, M. Arch. Accreditation Task Force from 2008 - 2010, and Robert James Eidlitz Fellowship since 1975.

Henry has also served on the following committees: Stein Institute Award in 2013, College Academic Integrity Hearing Board from 2006 - 2016, Diversity from 1971 - 2000, College of Architecture, Art and Planning Executive from 1978 - 1985, University Faculty Committee on Program Review from 2018

- 2021, University Faculty Senate Nominating Committee from 2016 – 2019, President Skorton's Think Tank on Linkages Between the United States and African Universities from 2018 – 2021, Cornell University's Academic Leadership Council from 1990 – 1999, Cornell University's Research and Outreach Council from 1995 – 2004 and an executive committee member for the Institute for African Development from 1972 to present.

Internationally, Henry was a member of the University Tenure and Promotion Committee and a member of the Education Review and Realignment Committee at King Fahd University of Petroleum and Minerals in Dhahran in Saudi Arabia from 1999 - 2000. He was an educational program reviewer and external tenure reviewer at the Department of Architecture at the University of Kuwait, Safat, Kuwait from 2000 - 2003. He was an external tenure reviewer at the Department of Architecture at the American University of Beirut in Lebanon in 2016 and an external reviewer at the School of Architecture and Planning at the Kwame Nkrumah University of Science and Technology in Kumasi, Ghana from 2002 – 2004.

Honors and Awards

Henry was a Walter Higgins Scholar at Cornell University from 1963 to 1969. He was awarded the Sands Medal by the Department of Architecture at Cornell University in 1968. He was an International Labor Organization Research Fellow for the United Nations Center for Housing, Building and Planning in New York in 1971. He was Honorary Fellow at the University of Cambridge Biographical Society in Cambridge, England in 1981. That same year Henry was also featured in "Who's who in the British Commonwealth". In 1989, he was given the Award of Excellence in Design by the Tompkins County Historic Society in Ithaca, New York. He won an Alumni Distinguished Teacher Award at Cornell University in 1990. He was a member of the Review and Selection

Committee for the United States National Academy of Sciences, University Linkage Program in Washington DC from 1995 to 1999.

Henry won the Faculty Innovation in Teaching Award at Cornell University in 2001 and the Distinguished Faculty-in-Residence Recognition Award in 2007. He has been a member of the Technical Review Committee of International Experts for Research Enrichment and Knowledge Exchange since 2015. He has been a member of the Wren Advisory Board, an independent think tank of experts in Architecture/Virtual Reality drawn from leading universities to promote the adoption of real-time experiential design and visualization since 2019.

Public and Community Service

Henry was a member of the Village of Cayuga Heights Planning Board from 2009 – 2013. He was a member of the Board of Trustees of Kendal Corporation in Ithaca in New York, and also a member of Rotary International Ithaca in New York, where he served as chair of several committees that sponsored community service programs from 1982 – 2000. Henry was a technical advisor to the Brown's Race Historic District Revitalization Committee in Rochester, New York from 1990 – 1998, and a member of Ithaca Landmarks and Preservation Committee from 1976 – 1995.

Family Life

Henry is married and has two children. He enjoys sports, photography, travel, multimedia production, classical music and jazz.

Professor Ebenezer Asafua Jackson

Early Years and Education

Ebenezer was born in Winneba on 23rd May, 1944. His parents were Daniel Kwesi Abbiw Jackson of the Royal Family of Senya Beraku and Joana Aba Yamoah from Winneba. Ebenezer is the last of six children. His older brothers, Abbiw, Joseph and Osborne, are featured elsewhere in this book. His father died when he was only five years old. So he was raised single-handedly by his mother. His mother was a trader in imported clothing, working as an agent with the United Africa Company, a British trading company. Ebenezer is eternally grateful to his mother for the sacrifices she made to raise him as a child all by herself.

Ebenezer had his elementary education at the Winneba Methodist Primary and Middle Schools. He won a scholarship to Mfantsipim Secondary School in Cape Coast in January 1957. He was Best Scholar of the Year 1963 in form 5, and also won the Shell Company award for Outstanding Advanced Level examination results in Ghana in 1963. He continued to the Kwame Nkrumah University of Science and Technology (KNUST) in Kumasi where he obtained his bachelor's and master's degrees in electrical engineering in 1967 and 1970 respectively. Ebenezer earned a diploma in management from Arthur D. Little Institute in Cambridge, USA in 1971. He obtained his doctorate in automatic control in the field of electrical engineering from the University of Pennsylvania, Philadelphia, in 1974. As a doctoral student, he was the African-American Institute Scholar at the University of Pennsylvania from 1970 through 1974.

Career Path

Ebenezer started his professional career as a teaching assistant in the Faculty of Engineering at the Kwame Nkrumah University of Science and Technology (KNUST) in Kumasi, while he was doing his master's degree at the university. On his return to the university after obtaining his doctorate in 1974, Ebenezer was successively lecturer, senior lecturer, associate professor and head of Department of Electrical and Computer Engineering in the School of Engineering. He was appointed dean of the School of Engineering in 2002 and held that position until his retirement in 2004.

Ebenezer was instrumental in introducing the Modular Course System and the Semester System at the university in 1977. The system is now being used in all the post-secondary institutions in the country. He was also the first to write the software for processing examination and providing transcript using Dbase III in the School of Engineering and then the entire university. The software is still the basis for examination reporting at the university.

While lecturing at KNUST, during his sabbaticals, Ebenezer also taught electrical engineering courses at the University of Lagos, the National University of Rwanda, Christian Service University College in Kumasi, and Kumasi Polytechnic. His research areas include control systems, energy and computers in education. He has over 55 publications in conference proceedings and journals. He has supervised undergraduate and graduate students writing their theses, and served as external examiner to the University of Ghana, the Regional Maritime University, the University of Mines and Technology and other polytechnics in Ghana. He has also served as a consultant to the Ghana Standards Board, several government ministries and the African Development Foundation.

As dean of the School of Engineering, Ebenezer introduced computer, petroleum, aerospace and telecommunications engineering programs into the School of Engineering. During his tenure, the school raised funds to complete the construction of a four-storey building which had staff offices and classrooms. He was also able to complete the Engineering Guest House which had been started six years earlier. The guest house is the most sought after campus housing by guests to the university, and a major income source for the School.

Ebenezer spent his 1995/96 sabbatical leave with the Volta River Authority, (VRA), the country's premier hydro-electric generating plant in Akosombo. While there, he helped develop guidelines on acquiring and operating energy-efficient appliances for the Authority. He also helped promote energy-efficient bulbs, which led to the widespread use of these bulbs and a ban on incandescent bulbs in the country. Ebenezer is a fellow of the Ghana Institution of Engineering, a member of the International Solar Energy Society and was a member of the Institution of Electrical and Electronic Engineers from 1974 – 1978.

Jackson Educational Complex

After retiring from the Kwame Nkrumah University of Science and Technology in 2004, Ebenezer continued to teach at the university on contract until 2010. He and his wife, Mrs. Theodosia Wilhelmina Jackson, founded the Jackson College of Education in 2009. The College became the nucleus of the Jackson Educational Complex which now includes other departments. The complex was the first and only private college of education using Distance Learning in the country. The college started with 284 students in its three-year associate degree program in Basic Education and currently has 6000 students. It had graduated a cumulative total of 12,300 students by December 2020.

Benevolence

What sets Ebenezer and his wife, Theodosia, apart from most, is their sense of commitment to the community. They recognise what God has enabled them to achieve. Consequently, they have committed themselves to helping not only the needy students in their educational complex but also the nearby towns and villages. The Jacksons instituted the Jackson and DEEN Foundations in April 2017 to oversee their charitable work. Within a three-year period, these two foundations have established a remarkable record of achievements.

The Jackson Foundation gives scholarships to students with special needs especially financial. It also awards scholarships for women empowerment, early childhood and French studies trainees. Early 2021, the Jackson College of Education commissioned a seven-unit classroom block at Danyame-Kwaem, a settler community near Obenimase in the Asante-Akim Central Municipality. This school was built for the villagers by the Rev. Emmanuel Dela Tega, a minister of the Presbyterian Church of

Ghana. This village is inhabited mostly by migrants from Ghana's northern regions who are engaged in cocoa farming.

The new classroom block is bringing renewed hope for hundreds of children who had been studying in an abandoned poultry farm. The abandoned poultry farm served as a makeshift classroom for over 200 children who could not walk a daily round trip of nine miles to go to school at Obenimase, the closest big village to the community. The school has since then being adopted by Mrs. Theodosia Jackson. The school was recently supplied with uniforms, shoes, food items and teaching materials. Two scholarships have also been awarded to students who have volunteered to teach at the school after completing their education at the Jackson School of Education.

The DEEN Foundation has provided cement and other materials for the construction of toilets at the Kumasi Central Prison. It has provided food, toiletries and laundry soap to the following institutions: the Manhyia Local Prison, the Ashanti Presbytery of the Ghana Presbyterian Church, Kumasi Metro Education Office, Ashanti Inter-School and Colleges Sports Federation, SOS Children's Village in Kumasi, Kwame Nkrumah University Junior High School. The foundation recently donated early childhood teaching materials to Sinapi Abi Micro Schools. During 2019 – 2020, the couple collaborated with former students from Amankwatia Middle High Junior High School at Asafo in Kumasi to renovate an old school building and provide new school supplies and equipment to the school. The above works have established the couple's reputation as one of Ghana's premier philanthropists.

Awards

The Jackson Educational Complex has received several awards over the years. It was awarded the Micjoy Award in 2014 for being Ghana's most influential private college of education. It also received the following awards in 2015: the Business Initiative Directions (BID) Award in Frankfurt, the Europe Business Assembly (EBA) Award in Montreux and the World Conference of Businesses (WORLDCOB) Award in Houston.

The Complex received the following awards in 2016: the African Quality Award in Kumasi, Ghana, World Business Assembly (WBA), and the Golden European Award in Dubai. It also received the following awards in 2017: World Confederation of Businesses (WORLDCOB), the second such award in Houston, and the African Quality Award, also the second, in Kumasi. Their foundations were awarded the Micjoy Award for their zeal to transform lives, and the Extraordinary Achievement Award by the National Philanthropy Forum, both in 2018. Other awards include the European Society for Quality Research (ESQR) in 2019, Quality Choice Prize and WORLDCOB Award in 2019 and 2020, and EBA Top 100 achievements in Science and Education in 2021.

At the personal level, Ebenezer has also received numerous awards. He was admitted as a member of the Oxford Academic Union by the Europe Business Assembly, (EBA), Montreux, Manager of the Year also by the EBA, World Leader Business Person by WORLDCOB, all in 2015. In 2016 he was awarded the World Business Assembly Certificate for Golden European Award for Quality and Business Prestige in Dubai. He also received the World Leader Business Person from WORLDCOB in 2017. He received the Marquis Lifetime Achievement Award for Unwavering Excellence in Education in 2018 and Manager of the Year by EBA in 2021.

Family Life

Ebenezer was raised a Methodist by his mother, an ardent Christian. As the Bible says "Train up a child the way he should go and even when he is old, he will not depart from it." Proverbs 22:6. As Ebenezer went through senior high school and at the university, he learned through the Scripture Union, that however gentle and humble he was, he was a sinner and had fallen short of the glory of God as stated in Romans 3: 23. He also got to know from Romans 6: 23 that the wages of sin is death, but the gift of God is eternal life in Christ Jesus. Hence, in his first year at the university in 1963, he asked Jesus Christ to be his personal Lord and Saviour. He has since been serving the Lord as a local preacher, a Society Steward, a leader in the Methodist Church and a patron to organizations in the church and other Christian groups.

For recreation, Ebenezer has been singing as a soloist and a choir member. He has produced a recording of a Gospel album called "The King is Coming". While a graduate student in the United States, he was a member of the Mendelsohn Club of Philadelphia and the Cleveland Orchestra Chorus which performed with the Philadelphia, Cleveland and New York Philharmonic orchestras at Carnegie and Avery Fisher Halls under the renowned conductors, Eugene Ormandy and Lorin Maazel. Ebenezer's five siblings are all academicians, excelling in the fields of mathematics and science. The three senior brothers are university professors in mathematics, all profiled above, while the eldest sister is a physiotherapist. The youngest sister is also a graduate in mathematics. He and Theodosia have four children, three males and a female. Two of the children are engineers, one a medical doctor and one is a pharmacist.

Professor Albert Odontoh Ebo Richardson

Early Life and Education

Albert Ebo Richardson, affectionately called Ebo by family members and numerous acquaintances in Ghana and around the world, was born on 22nd January, 1946 at Assin-Fosu in the Central Region of Ghana. His father, Joseph William Richardson (JWR), alias Kweku Amanyi, was from Winneba. His mother, the former Beatrice Freeman, alias Abena Essuon, was from Agona-Swedru, fifteen miles north of Winneba. Ebo's father, JWR, was from a line of Richardsons who had settled in Winneba from the Gomoa area in the Central Region in the 19th Century. The oldest of the three brothers is Henry William Richardson (HWR), alias Kobena Amanyi. Next is Joseph William Richardson (JWR), alias

Kweku Amanyi. The youngest is Albert William Richardson (AWR), alias Kobena Odontoh, originally "Dontoh". All three ended up working for the United Africa Company Ltd. (UAC). Working for UAC, HWR eventually settled in Nsawam, JWR in Cape Coast, and AWR in Half-Assini.

Ebo's father, as mentioned above, worked for the United Africa Company for 40 years, during which period he was transferred a few times from one town to another. However, Winneba is where the family considered home. Ebo grew up in a household filled with lots of children. He attended the African Methodist Episcopal Zion (AME Zion) School in Cape Coast. He went to Adisadel College, also in Cape Coast, in January 1960 with a Ghana Cocoa Marketing Board scholarship. In high school Sixth Form, Ebo passed his General Certificate of Education, Advanced Level examination, in physics, pure mathematics, additional mathematics and French. He was school Head Prefect in his final year, 1967.

While at Adisadel, Ebo played the Cello in the school symphonic orchestra. He was one of three student organists, a member of the Scripture Union, the school football team, and also served on the editorial board of the school magazine, "The Owl". It is clear that he was an all rounded student both in and out of the classroom. After finishing Adisadel in 1967, Ebo won an African Scholarship Program for American Universities (ASPAU) award for undergraduate studies at Yale University in New Haven, Connecticut.

Ebo got his bachelor's degree in engineering and applied science in 1971 from Yale. He obtained his master's in engineering (M.S.E.E.) degree in 1974 at Case Institute of Engineering at Case Western Reserve University in Cleveland, Ohio. While doing his masters degree, he served as a teaching assistant at the university. After a five-year stint in industry, he continued to Pennsylvania State University, University Park in Pennsylvania in 1978, where he obtained his doctorate in electrical engineering in 1983.

Career Path

Ebo started his professional career in 1973 as an Electronics Design Engineer with Polaroid Corporation in Cambridge, Massachusetts. He then worked with Digital Equipment Corporation in Maynard, Massachusetts in 1975, as senior engineer where he was a member of a group that designed, built and tested electronic circuits for state of the art disk drives. He entered academia in 1982 as lecturer in the Department of Electrical Engineering, University of Benin in Benin City in Nigeria.

After three years in Nigeria, Ebo returned to the United States and joined the Department of Electrical and Computer Engineering at Northeastern University in Boston, Massachusetts as assistant professor. He later transferred to the Department of Electrical Engineering at California State University (Cal State, Chico) in Chico in 1989, as associate professor. He was promoted to full professor with tenure in 1993. Ebo was appointed chair of the Department of Electrical and Computer Engineering at Cal State, Chico, in 2011. Later that year, he was made Professor Emeritus, and he retired.

Accomplishments

As a professor at California State University in Chico for 25 years, Ebo taught many undergraduate and graduate courses including the following: electronics, electrical engineering, microelectronics, semiconductor device physics and technology, digital systems design, microprocessor systems, embedded systems, computer architecture, assembly language and high-level language (C and C++), and senior project design and implementation. He also supervised the following laboratories: advanced digital systems, digital electronics and microprocessors, software and simulation tools and microelectronics fabrication and characterization.

Ebo was three times visiting professor at the University of Zacatecas in Mexico between 1992 and 2000. During the summer of 1997, he was visiting professor and researcher at North Dakota State University in Fargo, North Dakota. Between 1996 and 1998, he spent two 12-week summers as a faculty fellow at NASA/ASEE Johnson Space Center in Houston, Texas. From 1999 through 2004, he was co-project director for the Fund for the Improvement of Post Secondary Education (FIPSE). This was a program that involved managing staff, recruiting, supervising and advising engineering students from the university as well as other colleges.

Ebo was director of the North American Mobility Program, a program for collaboration and exchange of engineering students and faculty among six United States universities, two universities in Canada, Manitoba and Saskatchewan, and two universities in Mexico, Zacatecas and San Luis Potosi. The program was sponsored by the U. S. Department of Education. For the second phase of the project which lasted from 2007 to 2011, Ebo was the Principal Investigator as well as Project Director. From 1992 through 1994, Ebo was the supervising electronic design engineer for the HAZMAT Remote Controlled Vehicle, a project sponsored by the California Department of Transportation (CALTRANS). Ebo has presented many papers at numerous conferences and workshops.

Academic Committees

Ebo served on a task force to develop new syllabuses for combined computer science and computer engineering courses in 2009. He served as a member of committees responsible for departmental retention, tenure and promotion for the college. He also served as advisor for the university's chapter of the Engineering Honor Society of Tau Beta Pi. He was a member of the Department's group that wrote an Accreditation Report for the

Accreditation of Engineering and Technology. From 1994 through 1995, he helped recruit students for the College of Engineering at the university. He served in the Chico State Faculty Senate from 1991 to 1993 as the elected Faculty Senator from the College of Engineering, Computer Science and Construction Management. Ebo was a lifetime member of the Institute of Electrical and Electronic Engineers (IEEE), U. S. A.

Awards

At Ebo's promotion to full professor with tenure at Cal State, Chico, on 20th May, 1993, the citation read, "The significant contributions you have made to the instructional, research, and service programs of the University are greatly appreciated. Your rise to national prominence as a Scholar and a contributor to your chosen profession reflects well upon our community. The campus is enhanced by your presence and we look forward to your continued success as a leader in higher education." On 2nd May 1994, the university awarded him the "Professional Achievement Honor, for Significant Contributions to Your Field of Endeavor". Then in August 2012, the university awarded him "Professor Emeritus of Electrical and Computer Engineering", recognizing the outstanding and meritorious professional and personal contributions to the growth of the University and its students.

Community Service

Ebo was an active member of the following groups: the Yale University Alumni Association, the 1965 Class of Adisadel College, the Mpunto (social and economic improvement) Club of Agona and Gomoa Districts in Ghana, and the Ghanaian Association of Sacramento (GAS). He was a regular financial contributor to the above groups and causes. He annually supported the following institutions as well: the Ashesi University in Ghana, the "100 Foundations in Education" based in Atlanta, elementary and middle school educational programs in Ghana, and the Endowment Fund for Agona-Swedru Methodist School in Ghana. He was a member of the African Students Association of Yale University (1967 – 1971), and a member of the African Association of Greater Cleveland, Ohio (1971 – 1973). He has been an advisor and mentor to the African community in Chico since 1989. From 1989 through 2014, he was Faculty Advisor and mentor to student members of "Africa Club" at Cal State, Chico.

Ebo received awards for his involvement in and support for these community groups. In 2016, he was given the "Recognition as One of the Founding Fathers" by the Ghana Association of Greater Boston on the occasion of the 25th anniversary of the group in Boston, Massachusetts. In 2011, he was given an award for "Strong Support, Sponsorship and Reliable Patronizing of Functions and Activities" by the Ghanaian "Ebusua Club" of San Francisco Bay area. In July 2010, he was given the "R. T. Orleans-Pobee Fellow" award for service to Adisadel College, his alma mater, Cape Coast, Ghana.

One of Ebo's most cherished awards was from the National Executive Committee of the Adisadel Old Boys Association (AOBA) of Ghana, which conferred on him "The AOBA Outstanding Santaclausian of the Year Award 2018". The Citation for that award, stated, among other things, that "You have made Adisadel College proud in your scientific and engineering achievements in the global academic community, particularly in the United States of America, after your record-breaking successes at your alma mater. In recog-nition of your selfless contribution to Santaclausian causes, and singular devotion to Adisadel College in particular, the National Executive Committee of the Adisadel Old Boys Association (AOBA) of Ghana, confers on you The AOBA Outstanding Santaclausian of The Year Award, 2018".

Active Community Engagement

Ebo's community involvement was not only in the form of passive and hands-off donations of money to organizations and institutions. Ebo donated equipment to the University of Cape Coast, and also worked with the university's School of Physical Sciences to develop a new Embedded Systems Laboratory for equipping students with hands-on, employable, technical skills. Ebo gave guest lectures on Embedded Systems Laboratory Development during short visits to the University of Cape Coast, and also to the School of Engineering Science at the University of Ghana, Legon.

Ebo also donated equipment and microcontrollers for an Embedded Systems Laboratory to Legon. Ebo teamed up with three other Ghanaian engineers and scientists, resident in the United States, to form a foundation named AYASPAU. The foundation purchased two hundred new engineering textbooks to the School of Engineering Science at the University of Ghana, Legon. With the donation of those new textbooks, a new Engineering Reference Library was established for engineering students and faculty. The foundation also provided a scholarship for a biomedical graduate student for two years at the School of Engineering Sciences at the University of Ghana, Legon. Ebo also served as the chairman of the International Scientific Advisory Board (ISAB) for an engineering program at the Kwame Nkrumah University of Science and Technology (KNUST), in Kumasi, Ghana. The program called KEEP (KNUST Engineering Education Program), is a World Bank initiative for the improvement of postgraduate education.

During the 1970s and 1980s, Ebo worked with a group of science and engineering graduates from Ghana, the Cameroons, the Democratic Republic of the Congo, Nigeria and Kenya, who were employed in the high-technology industries in the Boston-Cambridge area in Massachusetts. The group aimed at fostering the development of these industries in their native countries.

Most of the members subsequently returned home to their respective African countries and made substantial contributions towards building a scientific and technological base for development. Those who remained in the US continued to engage with their home countries through frequent visits to collaborate with their counterparts in Africa.

In recent years, Ebo continued to work with Diasporan groups who desire to contribute towards bridging the gap between Ghana and the advanced industrialized countries. The group's efforts culminated in a one-week conference in 2019 at Peduase Lodge in Aburi, near Accra, under the auspices of the Ghana Institution of Engineering. This conference brought together over a hundred members of academia and those involved in industry from both Ghana and elsewhere. The conference was addressed by President Nana Akuffo Addo and ended with several initiatives with the universities and the private sector that would help create manufacturing hubs to commercialize Ghana's scientific and technological inventions.

Family Life

Ebo was married to the former Cecilia Yankson and has three children, Kojo Essuon (in health care industry), Afua Amanyiwa (in dentistry), and Elvert Bayin (in health & human resources). He enjoyed traveling, playing the organ, listening to classical and choral music as well as the traditional Ghanaian hi-life music. He passed late November 2021.

Professor John Humphrey Amuasi

Early Years and Education

John was born in Winneba on 29th January, 1946 to Henry Emmanuel Amuasi, famously called Papa Amos, and the former Madam Elizabeth Paintsil. He is the seventh of ten children. He started his elementary education at the Winneba Methodist Primary School at age six. He spent class four at Besease Methodist Primary School when his older sister, Isabella Okorba Essilfie, with whom he was living, was transferred to Besease as a domestic science teacher. He passed the Common Entrance examination when he was in middle form three. This took him to Ghana National College in Cape Coast from 1960 through 1967. He was appointed boys' head prefect in Lower Six. He continued to the University of Ghana, Legon in 1967/68 as a physics/geology major. He left after one year for the Kwame Nkrumah University of Science and Technology in Kumasi where he got his bachelor's degree in physics in June 1973.

Career Path

John joined the Ghana Atomic Energy Commission as scientific assistant in December 1974. He got a United Kingdom Technical Assistance scholarship to study for his master's degree in radiation physics. He obtained his doctorate in medical physics at the Institute of Cancer Research at the Royal Marsden Hospital, the University of London, in the United Kingdom. John returned to Ghana in February 1982, and went back to the Atomic Energy Commission where he was promoted to scientific officer. In that position, he was assigned to the Korle Bu Teaching Hospital as clinical medical physicist. From 1984 through 1986, he was a post-doctoral fellow at the Institute of Nuclear Medicine and Medical Physics of the University of Florence in Italy with a grant from the Abdus Salam International Center for Theoretical Physics, Trieste.

John was promoted to senior scientific officer at the Commission on his return to Ghana in 1986. He became principal scientific officer in 1991. He served as head of the Department of Physics and Reactor Technology from 1989 through 1992. He was elected scientific staff representative and member of the Interim Management Committee of the Ghana Atomic Energy Commission and served from 1989 – 1992.

John was appointed secretary of the Commission in 1994, after acting in that position for one year. The position was re-designated as the Executive Secretary in 1996, and then re-designated again as the Director-General in 2001 when the new Act 588 of 2000 was passed by parliament. In effect, Professor Amuasi became the Chief Executive Officer of the Ghana Atomic Energy Commission, the highest position at the Commission, effective 1993 until 2003. He retired in 2006, after 32 years with the Commission.

After his retirement, John was reengaged and appointed coordinator, director, and dean of the newly established Graduate School of Nuclear and Allied Sciences, which was affiliated with the University of Ghana, Legon, and located at the Atomic Campus in Accra. He also lectured full-time from 2006 – 2016 at the Medical Physics Department at the school, and later part-time from 2017 - 2021. He was also a supervisor and an examiner of master's and Ph.D. students' theses.

While working at the Ghana Atomic Energy Commission, John, in his capacity as the National Liaison Officer, worked with the Technical Cooperation Department of the International Atomic Energy Agency (IAEA) as consultant and provided technical assistance to the country. He and the chairman of the GAEC succeeded in getting Ph.D. sandwich programs for the GAEC staff in various research disciplines including research reactor utilization, nuclear power program, gamma irradiation, nuclear medicine and radiotherapy. He also served as an International Atomic Energy Agency consultant on nuclear medicine to Uganda, Tanzania, Tunisia, Sierra Leone, Zambia, Senegal, Libya and Vienna.

Achievements

John has served on several IEA task force and technical working group meetings. The first task force was set up by the International Atomic Energy Agency to explore avenues for "Participation with African Member States: Areas of Possible Improvement in Technical Assistance Cooperation (TAC) Matters". In 2007, John served on another task force on "Human Resource Development and Nuclear Knowledge Management" in Tripoli, Libya. Other task forces he served on were the following: "Sustaining the Managerial Capability of AFRA Member States", the "African

Regional Cooperative Agreement for Research Development and Training on Nuclear Science and Technology", and "Regional Postgraduate Medical Physics Syllabus for Academic Programs for African Universities".

John was a member of the delegations to the International Atomic Energy Agency Vienna Annual General Conferences from the 37th Session in 1993 to the 46th Session in 2002. He served as an alternate governor at the IAEA Board of Governors' meeting on three occasions, between 1994 and 2002. He was a member of the National Radiotherapy and Nuclear Medicine Committee from 1994 through 2003. He was a member of the IAEA Standing Advisory Group on Nuclear Applications (SAGNA) from 2004 – 2009.

John was also an external examiner for Kwame Nkrumah University of Science and Technology and the University of Ghana, Legon, for several years. John was a Regular Associate Member of the International Center for Theoretical Physics, TRIESE, from 1986 – 1993 and a Senior Associate Member from 2000 – 2007. He was a foundational president of the Ghana Society for Medical Physics (GSMP) and served from 2011 through 2017. Currently he is a Fellow of the Ghana Institute of Physics.

During John's tenure as chief executive of the Ghana Atomic Energy Commission, he participated in the commissioning of the 30 KW Miniature Neutron Source Reactor, the 1.85 PBq multi-purpose pilot scale Gamma Irradiation Facility, the Health Physics and Radioactive Waste Management Center, the National Center for Mathematical Sciences, the National Radiotherapy and Nuclear Medicine Center, and the old Act 204 of 1963, which established the Commission and the subsequent new Act 588 of 2000.

Over the course of his career, John has supervised several doctoral students. One of his students was adjudged the International Union of Pure and Applied Physics "Young Scientist of the Year" in 2016, in the category of medical physics. The award was established by the International Organization of Medical Physics for the best performing young medical physics scientist below the age of 40. The student also won the Best Poster Presentation Award when he participated in the maiden University of Ghana Doctoral Conference in 2015.

John has published one book, "The History of Ghana Atomic Energy Commission: 40 Years of Nuclear Science and Technology Applications in Ghana" (2004). He and his wife, Joyce, contributed two chapters in a book entitled, "Pre-Marital Preparation and Counseling." He has also authored and co-authored about 60 articles in academic journals, written 17 technical reports and attended several workshops and conferences all over the world.

Awards

John has received several awards: Order of the Volta-Officer on July 3, 2008, Meritorious Award on the occasion of the Atomic Energy Commission's 50th anniversary in 2013, Meritorious Award for his service on the Governing Council of the Trinity Theological Seminary at Legon in 2015, and an award by the Allied Health Profession Council in 2016. John was honored by the International Atomic Energy Agency in collaboration with the Ghana Atomic Energy Commission on 9th July, 2018, in recognition of his "outstanding services and exceptional achievements in driving the Ghana Atomic Energy Commission to heights of excellence".

Charitable Work

John is a board member of the Rafiki Foundation. He and his wife, Joyce, are very actively involved in the work of this foundation in Ghana. The Rafiki Foundation is headquartered at Eustis, Florida, in the United States. The foundation was introduced into Ghana by the Bible Study Fellowship in Accra in 1989. The foundation provides services to orphans and is currently operating in Ethiopia, Uganda, Tanzania, Kenya, Liberia, Nigeria, Malawi, Rwanda and Ghana. It supports missionaries who work alongside locals in these countries. Under the executive directorship of Mrs. Rosemary Jensen, the foundation formed an alliance with the Methodist Church Ghana.

The alliance between the Methodist Church and the Foundation has resulted in two projects in Ghana. The first project is the Rafiki Children Center at Agyen-Kotoku, a suburb of Accra. This was the first project in Africa to be established by the Foundation. The second project is an orphanage, known as the Methodist-Rafiki Satellite Village at Gyaahadze, a village a few miles east of Winneba. The Rafiki Children Center at Agyen-Kotoku has 250 pupils with 75 accommodated at the center. The rest come from nearby villages to be educated at the school. Five of their graduates will be going to universities starting 2021-2022 academic year. Eight of the graduates have already graduated from universities in Ghana. The Orphanage at Gyaahadze has 49 pupils from pre-school to junior high school. Ten of their graduates are currently (May 2021) at Mfantsipim and Mfantseman high schools. Five will be graduating into universities for the first time starting the 2021-2022 academic year.

Family Life

At the personal level, John grew up in a Methodist family and environment and became a Christian in February 1969 during a Christian Mission Crusade organized by the University Christian Fellowship at the Kwame Nkrumah University of Science and Technology in Kumasi (KNUST). During his student years at the university, John, and fellow student Christians, spent Sunday afternoons visiting villages and secondary schools in and around Kumasi sharing the Good News of Christ's salvation message with the villagers and the young students.

John sang in the Male Voice Choir and the University Interdenominational Church Choir at the University and was vice president of the University Christian Fellowship during the1971-72 academic year. John has been a member of the Mount Sinai Methodist Society at Atomic in Accra for several years. He is a Bible Class leader, a choir master, a lay preacher and chairman of the counseling team at the church.

John is also a member of the Accra Evening Men's Bible Class. He has held the following positions in several Christian organizations: a member of the board of directors of the Bible Study Fellowship (BSF) from 2007 – 2019, with the headquarters in San Antonio, Texas, member of the governing council of the Trinity Theological Seminary from 2008 – 2015, member of the Marriage Counseling Committee of the Methodist Church Ghana, and member of the Connexional (national) Liturgy Committee also of the Methodist Church since 2019.

John married his high school sweetheart, the former Joyce Eshun, at the Winneba Ebenezer Methodist Church on July 28, 1974. They have been blessed with five children, three boys and two girls and several grandchildren. The children are Henry (a biophysicist in Holland), John Humphrey, Jr. (a senior lecturer in Public Health at the KNUST), Ebenezer (director of International Relations, Wisconsin International University College in Accra), Grace-Joy (teacher at the Anglogold Ashanti International School in Obuasi) and Mercy (Manager, Counseling Psychology Center at the GAEC).

Section C
The Professionals

Mr. Sam Mensah Herbert Baxter Yarney

Early Years

S am Yarney was born on 16th May, 1894 in Winneba, the third of eleven children. His parents were Joseph Haveluck Yarney and the former Jane Annobil. Sam attended Winneba Methodist Infant and Senior Schools.

Career Path

Sam taught at the Winneba Methodist School after completing middle school. He took English and other classes at the then College of Preceptors, now defunct. Sam later joined the Judicial Service in Accra and served as court registrar and interpreter from the mid-1920s. He was transferred to Northern Region to work in the Regional Co-Ordinating Council. His rank at the time is not known. However, judging from the fact that he was transported in a sedan chair from one district capital to the next until he finally reached Tamale, it is most likely that he was a high ranking civil servant. While in Tamale, which was the capital city of the Northern Region at the time, he learned to speak both Hausa and Dagomba. His mastery of these two dialects made it very easy for him to work with the local chiefs, workers and the people in the area.

Career Achievements

Sam served as a member of a committee that was set up to define the western, northern and eastern boundaries of the then Gold Coast. He was later transferred to Kumasi, Koforidua and Cape Coast within the Co-Ordinating Council.

In the late 1940s, Sam was tasked with helping establish the first local government training school at Sabon Zongo in Accra. After that initial assignment, he was asked to set up a similar institution in Tamale. He was appointed a local court magistrate for the Winneba High Court in 1963 and he served until 1967. He also served on the Gomoa-Awutu-Effutu-Senya District Council. His final official position was as chairman of the board of governors for Winneba Secondary School.

Sam as a Musician

Sam showed an interest in music at a very young age. His father was a musician so he had his first music lessons from his father. He took correspondence courses with the Victoria College of Music to advance his knowledge of music. He was recommended for the position of external examiner for the Victoria College of Music, London, responsible for students in all of West Africa who wanted to learn music. However, his transfer to Tamale at the time prevented him from accepting that position. His friend and fellow musician, Professor Percy J. Mensah, was chosen for that position. Sam served briefly as the choirmaster and organist of the Winneba Ebenezer Methodist Church during the early 1920s. Sam was a prolific composer. He composed over 200 hymn tunes, voluntaries, marches, canticles and vespers. His tunes celebrated important events in the lives of his friends and members of the Winneba Methodist Church. He never formally established a music school but he taught young people to play the piano wherever he was stationed. During his retirement years, music students from Winneba, often consulted him for advice and instruction. He died on 29th May, 1976 leaving an indelible mark on Church music in Ghana.

Mr. Oman Ghan Blankson

Early Life and Education

Oman Ghan Blankson was born on 17th November, 1899. His parents were Richard John Blankson and Hannah Roberts. He lost his father when he was only seven years old. He was the fourth of five children, three boys and two girls. The first and second children, R. A. H. Blankson and Matilda Blankson were prominent business professionals. The third child was the Reverend Kodwo Abbam Blankson, a Methodist Minister and the first secretary of the then Gold Coast Methodist Synod. The fifth and last was Mrs. Adelina Mills-Robertson, a Methodist local preacher and one-time president of the Winneba Ebenezer Methodist Women's Fellowship.

Upon completing his elementary school education at the Winneba Methodist Primary and Middle Schools in 1917, Oman taught at the middle school for seven years. He then took up bookkeeping and worked successively with Messrs Millers Brothers,

East Trading Company and finally with the United Africa Company at Winneba and Swedru.

Life as a Musician

Oman's interest in music began when he was in elementary school. His headmaster, the Rev. S. C. Dodd, noticed his clear singing voice during school singing classes. Rev. Dodd persuaded Oman's mother, Hannah Roberts, to have him join the Winneba Methodist Church Choir. His interest in music blossomed from then on. Since there were no music schools in the country at the time, Oman, like many of his contemporaries, took correspondence courses with the Victoria College of Music in London. The college had musicians in the country who supervised the practical sections of the courses. Three of those tutors were Rev. Attoh Ahumah, Charles E. Graves, and Percy J. Mensah. Oman obtained his associate certificates A. VCM and A mus. VCM through those courses.

Oman was appointed organist and choir master of the Winneba Methodist Church in 1920 when he was only 21 years old. He started composing hymn tunes two years later. His first composition was motivated by the death of one of his choris-ters, Kofi Bonney. This was followed by other compositions which celebrated weddings, births and deaths involving his family and friends and also for the church. The Rev. Albert Benjamin Dickson wrote most of the lyrics to Oman's hymn tunes. A few of the lyrics were written by friends including the Rev. Gaddiel R. Acquaah, Rev. Charles D. Kittoe and E. O. Tetteh.

As choir director, Oman initiated and conducted a choir festival at the Winneba Methodist Church during the 1940s. This event was so popular that the church decided to celebrate the festival every year. Oman also travelled throughout the country to conduct singing competitions. He also founded a music school to teach young boys and girls music and organ playing. In all, he composed over 120 hymn tunes, chants and anniversary songs. His music compositions are very melodic, hence their popularity. In 1949, he published "The Robertsville Hymnal" which he dedicated to his mother, Hannah Roberts. According to the late Professor Emeritus J. H. Kwabena Nketiah, ethnomusicologist of worldwide fame and former professor at the School of Music at the University of Ghana, Legon and the University of California at Los Angeles, this was the first formal music publication by an African at the time.

Legacy

Oman's music compositions, especially "Frank: Da Yie, Dɔfo Fonafo" are sung whenever Ghanaians meet for funerals both in Ghana and elsewhere. This tune is also played at Ghana's state funerals by the Ghana Military Band. One of his hymn tunes "Alpha et Omega: Beloved, Let Us Love" has even been adopted by Susanna Wesley Mission Auxiliary, a woman's organization in the United Kingdom as its anthem. Also 16 of his hymn tunes have been added to the "New Methodist Christian Asɔr Ndwom" which was published in 2010. In recognition of his outstanding contributions to the spiritual life of the Methodist Church through his music, his plaque has been displayed at the entrance to the Winneba Ebenezer Methodist Church. The Winneba Municipal Authority has honored him by naming a street in Winneba after him.

Oman passed on his music skills to his children and several others whom he taught at his music school. Notable among them are Mr. Africanus Abaka Wilson, who has been the organist at Kenton Methodist Church in Harrow, London, since 2004, and Kofi Nyansah Koomson, former music lecturer at the Advanced Teacher Training College in Winneba. All his children are musicians in one way or another. Those who could not play the piano were gifted with rich singing voices.

Family Life

Oman retired as the organist and choirmaster of the Winneba Ebenezer Methodist Church in 1952 when he became blind. At his passing in October 1974, Oman was survived by his wife of 47 years, the former Jane NaYɛNa Arthur, and eleven children, eight boys and three girls. The eldest was the late Mrs. Elsie Quaison-Sackey, the wife of Ghana's first permanent representative to the United Nations during the 1960s. Elsie is profiled in this book.

Mr. William Freebody Acquah

William, also known as Kofi Kine, was the grandson of Nana Ghartey IV, Omanhen of the Effutu State during the late 1890s. William may have been born either in the late 1890s or early 1900s, being a contemporary of Sam Yarney and Oman Ghan Blankson. His mother was Maame Rose Araba Nkuma. William was a catechist of the Winneba Methodist Church and served at Nsuekyir, Kweikrom and Afransi. He was a teacher and also served as secretary to the chief. Very little is known about his background, parents or education.

William was an organist and a composer. He wrote very popular musicals and cantatas that were performed by members of the Winneba Methodist Church. One of his famous musicals was based on King Solomon's life as recorded in 1 Kings, chapters 3 and 10. These passages tell the story of King Solomon, whose wisdom was legendary and known all over the Eastern world. This fame brought the queen of Sheba to Jerusalem to witness Solomon's fame for herself. Solomon's wisdom was demonstrated in his ability to discern who the true mother of the surviving baby of the two quarreling prostitutes was. This cantata was performed several times by groups within the Winneba Methodist Church.

In his later years William converted to Mosano Disco Christo Church (M.D.C.C.) where he continued composing and directing other musicals.

At his passing, he was survived by his wife, Mrs. Esther Acquah and five children.

Mr. Robert Herbert Blankson

Early Life and Education

Robert or Uncle Kwame, as he was commonly known, was born on 17th October, 1922. His parents were Robert Anaman Herbert Blankson and Madam Hannah Krampah, alias Arabah Apreba. Robert Anaman Herbert Blankson was the senior brother of Oman Ghan Blankson who is profiled above. Young Robert had his primary and middle school education at the Wesleyan School at Senya Beraku, Government Boys' School at Akim Oda and Methodist School in Winneba. He attended Accra Academy where he successfully completed the senior Cambridge Certificate in 1945.

Career Path

Robert joined the Information Services Department of the then Gold Coast Civil Service in 1946 as a mobile cinema interpreter. Those days, as part of the country's mass education program, the department sent out mobile vans to towns and villages to explain government policies, using newsreels and documentaries. In 1948, Robert joined the United Africa Company (UAC) where he later became manager. As manager of the company, Robert worked in Kumasi, Akim Oda, Obuasi, Bibiani, Konongo and Wa.

Robert left the UAC in 1958 to work with the newly established Ghana National Trading Corporation (GNTC) soon after the country attained independence. He left GNTC to work with United Company, Ltd., a private company. After two years with this company, he left and founded four companies, namely Herbert & Partners, Unique Parts Limited, Coir Fiber Processing Company and Ebelt Hooper Perfumery, with some friends. The last company manufactured talcum powder and other confectionery products in Accra. Robert and a friend, Mr. Hayford, had a fabrics store at Makola Market in Accra which they called Blankford, a combination of their last names.

Family Life

Robert was a Christian and served the Methodist Church faithfully, starting as a chorister in his youth. He helped found the Winneba Methodist Old Boys and Girls Association. He served as chairman at many of the church's harvest festivals and contributed financially towards many projects in the church. One of his lasting benevolences was a lectern, a small pulpit, that he donated to the Winneba Ebenezer Methodist Church. He died on 5th March 1974, leaving behind a large family.

Mr. Samuel Andoh Bannerman

Early Years and Education

S amuel was born in Winneba on 20th June, 1924. His home name was Kofi Kupa. He was the second child of nine children to Opanyin Kow Bannerman of the Royal Asona Ebusua of Ekumfi Ebram and Otuam and Ms. Elizabeth Wallice, also known as Maame Adwoa Mensema, of the Chief Annobil Anona Ebusua of Winneba. Sam attended the Winneba Methodist Mixed School and moved to Cape Coast to live with his Uncle, the late Rev. Albert Benjamin Dickson, then head of the Methodist Church in Cape Coast. Sam gained admission to Mfantsipim Secondary School in 1942 and completed form five in 1947.

Career Path

After Mfantsipim, Sam taught at the Winneba Methodist Middle School for two years. He then went to Accra where he worked with the Standard Bank of West Africa, now Standard Chartered Bank. He left later to work at the Ministry of Information where he was posted to Radio Ghana, now the Ghana Broadcasting Corporation, as program assistant. Sam worked for one year in Cape Coast then was transferred to Kumasi where he was in charge of the Ashanti and Brong Ahafo Regions for three years. In 1963, Sam and ten other broadcasters were sent to Britain to train in television production. This was followed by another three-month training at the Ryerson Institute in Toronto, Canada. He did practical training with the Communications and Broadcasting Corporation's regional station in Halifax, Nova Scotia. Sam was appointed director of television at the Ghana Broadcasting Corporation in 1975 and retired in 1983.

Family Life

Sam was a Christian, hardworking and soft-spoken. He died in 2007, leaving behind his wife, nine children and several grandchildren.

Mrs. Elsie Annie Quaison-Sackey

Early Years and Education

Elsie was born on Sunday, 18th December, 1927 at Winneba. She was the first of eleven children born to Oman Ghan Blankson, featured above, and the former Jane Aba NaYɛNa Arthur. Although Elsie was born on a Sunday, her name was changed from Esi to Ekua at the request of her father's aunt, Annie Blankson (Ekua Anamoaba), who had been blessed with five sons but no daughters.

Elsie grew up at Robertsville, her paternal family home in Winneba. As a young school girl, Elsie was very close to her father. Her father would teach her to sing many of his compositions as he wrote them. She was gifted with a melodic voice. Later in life, Elsie often wondered why her father never taught her, or her two younger sisters, how to play the piano or organ. This was quite intriguing, given that her brothers, eight of them after her, were all given music instruction and could play the piano with varying degrees of success.

Elsie attended Methodist Primary and Middle schools from 1933 to 1942. In 1943, she was admitted to Wesley College in Kumasi. After obtaining her teacher's certificate, she taught at Mmofratro in Kumasi, a Methodist School for girls. She later transferred to Wesley Girls High School in Cape Coast where she taught for four years. In 1950, she was awarded a scholarship to study for her diploma in education at the Norwich Teachers Training College, which was then affiliated with Cambridge University.

Career Path

In June 1952, after completing her diploma in education, with distinction, Elsie returned to the Gold Coast where she taught at the Methodist Primary School and later at the Methodist Girls School, both in Winneba. After a few years, she was transferred to Nyakrom Methodist School, where she was made headmistress of the school.

Elsie got married to Alex Quaison-Sackey on 7th April, 1951 at the Park Lane Methodist Church in Norwich, while she was a student at the Norwich Teachers Training College. As the wife of a diplomat, Elsie and Alex travelled extensively when Alex was transferred from one country to another on diplomatic assignments. The tours of Alex's diplomatic duties included Second Secretary at the Ghana High Commission in London, and later as Ghana's ambassador to the United Nations, ambassador to Cuba, Mexico and Brazil and finally as Ghana's Foreign Minister. Elsie travelled to several countries including Argentina, Brazil, Romania, and France. All the geography lessons she had taken in school came alive to her during these travels.

After the coup d'etat on 24th February, 1966, which overthrew President Kwame Nkrumah's government, Elsie returned to Ghana. She taught at the Winneba Preparatory School, Morning Star School and the Armed Forces Primary School, the latter two in Accra. It was while she was teaching at the Armed Forces Primary School that her health struggles began. She was diagnosed with myasthena gravis, a rare neurological disease that affected the elasticity of her muscles. This disease left her virtually paralyzed.

Family Life

She underwent major surgery in London in 1972 for her condition which improved her mobility a bit. In 1979, Elsie underwent another procedure at the National Institute of Health at Bethesda which enabled her to stand and walk. After the procedure, she was almost back to her normal healthy self and was able to travel all by herself on Amtrak from Washington, D.C. to Maryland, Virginia, Pennsylvania, Ohio, Colorado, Chicago, Utah and California, visiting family and friends.

It was during her late sixties that Elsie began to lose her eyesight. Elsie was a lifelong Methodist who knew her Bible very well. She loved to sing, and knew almost all the great hymns in the Methodist Hymn Book. When family and friends visited her at Akumbia Lodge and later at Anamoaba Fie, she would sing hymns with them and study the Bible with them as well. Her hobbies were crocheting and reading, but her favorite past time was playing Scrabble.

Elsie and Alex were blessed with six children. At her passing on 18th January, 2003, she left behind four of her children, Awo Aferba, K. B., Nenyi Embi and Yaaba, three grandchildren, Awenate, Kodwo Sei, and Nana Anamoaba, six brothers, two sisters, several cousins, nephews, nieces and in-laws.

Mr. Mark Napoleon Kweku Budu-Manuel

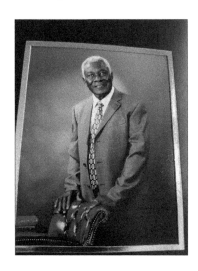

Early Life and Education

Kweku Budu-Manuel was born in Winneba on 19th March, 1928. His parents were Opanyin Samuel Kweku Annan Manuel of Anona Family at Ojobi and Madam Mary Johnson, alias Maame Adwoa Mensah of the Royal Nsona Family of Ekumfi traditional area. Opanyin Samuel Kweku Annan Manuel was a mason and contractor and Maame Adwoa Mensah traded in fabrics. Kweku was the first male child after six female siblings.

Kweku started school when he was six years old at the Winneba Zion Primary School, which was housed in his uncle's cocoa warehouse. After less than a year at the school, he was sent to Sekondi to live with his uncle, George Fynn, a postmaster. Kweku continued his elementary school education in Secondi, completing middle school standard seven at St. Peter's Elementary School. He enlisted in the Gold Coast Army in 1945, but pulled out soon after enlisting, much to the relief of his parents and siblings.

Career Path

Kweku worked briefly with the Union Trading Company (UTC) in Sekondi, before joining Elder Dempster Lines, a shipping company, where he worked as a stenographer. At the time of leaving the company, ten years later, he had risen to the rank of manager in the Manifest Department. The company moved its headquarters to Tema where a new port had been built. In 1958, at age 30, Kweku left the shipping company to work with the Ghana Broadcasting Corporation. He joined the Fantse Department where he was a newsreader. This was when he dropped his middle name, Napoleon. He reasoned that the name, Napoleon, did not quite fully reflect his Akan roots for someone working in a department that was charged with projecting the Ghanaian culture and norms. Kweku always started his segment with "Mara Kweku Budu na merekasa yi" meaning "It is me, Kweku Budu, speaking". His deep and clear voice resonated very well.

Apart from the newsreading, Kweku also did documentaries on farms, fisheries and other areas of interest. He headed three programs that were very popular with listeners: "Kodzi" "Tabon Mbo" and "Suo Wo Mfe". At one time the Fantse Department had luminaries like Kweku Acquaah, Kodwo Halm, Kobena Micah, Kobena Taylor and Marian Addy also known as Ama Sesaako, all of whom hailed from Winneba. Also at the Ghana Broadcasting Corporation, but in the English News Reading Department, was David Ghartey-Tagoe, also from Winneba.

Family Life

Kweku's hobbies included singing, which he relished with his deep baritone voice. He sang in Saint Andrew Anglican Church Choir in Sekondi. He was also a member of the Sekondi Minstrel Choir, a male voice choir boasting one hundred members. He loved cooking and playing soccer. He loved to organize get-togethers where friends took turns cooking. His specialty was corned beef jollof rice. His dress sense was impeccable. As a young man in his twenties, Kweku played with the Sekondi Hassacas football team.

Kweku was deeply religious throughout his life. He was a member of the Adabraka Methodist Church for several years before moving to Dansoman, where he worshipped at the newly founded Mt. Olivet Methodist Church. He was one of the founding members of the Men's Fellowship and served one term as the group's chaplain. He was a class leader. He also served on several church committees including Pastor-Parish Relations. He was chairman and spokesperson of the Royal Nsona Family of Ekumfi. His peaceful demeanor, patience, thought-provoking anecdotes and jokes endeared him to all who were privileged to work with him.

Kweku died on 3rd August, 2004, leaving behind his widow, the former Violet Adelina Mills-Robertson, eight children and seventeen grandchildren.

Mr. David Kweku Ghartey-Tagoe

Early Years and Education

G hartey-Tagoe was born on 13th March, 1929 in Koforidua. Both his parents, David Ghartey-Tagoe, Senior and Madam Mercy Efua Owu Mensah, were from Winneba. He was named after his father, David Ghartey-Tagoe. Senior David was an accountant with the United Africa Company and worked at the company's offices in the Gold Coast and Sierra Leone. Senior David left the company to go into private business as a timber merchant. He later became director of the then Timber Marketing Board. After retiring from the timber industry, he worked as an accountant at the Avenida Hotel in Accra. Young David's mother, Madam Mercy, was a seamstress, a baker and a trader, all at the same time. This was typical of hardworking and industrious mothers who were housewives.

Young David started his education at the Methodist Primary and Middle Schools in Winneba and passed the Standard Seven School final examination. He continued to Mfantsipim where he completed his secondary school education and acquired the Cambridge School and the London University Matriculation certificates. David then went to Wesley College in Kumasi where he obtained his Post-Secondary Teacher's certificate. David attended Dalhousie University in Canada in 1964, before enrolling at the University of Cape Coast as a mature student. He graduated in 1970 with a bachelor's degree in education, geography and English from the University. He also studied at Syracuse University where he obtained a certificate in broadcasting. He did refresher courses and training with the Canadian Broadcasting Corporation, the Voice of America, the British Broadcasting Corporation and the Center for Educational Television Overseas in London, while working with the Ghana Broadcasting Corporation.

Career Path

David started his professional career as a teacher. He taught for three years at Wesley College Practice School and seven years at Apam Secondary School. His subjects were geography, mathematics, English and Latin. At age 32, David joined the fledgling Ghana Broadcasting Corporation (GBC). His first assignment at GBC was as a radio producer-news reader. He rose through the ranks, becoming a television newscaster, producer-director, head of television programs, deputy director of television and then director of Television Unit. As director-general, his last position with GBC, apart from overseeing all the divisions including programming, David was instrumental in helping develop documentaries on high-ranking individuals and institutions and designing programs for schools and colleges.

David was an English language examiner for the West African Examinations Council from 1972 to 1975. He taught classes at the Schools of Performing Arts and Communication Studies at the University of Ghana, Legon, from 1977 to 1980, and from 1990 to 1999 respectively. He also taught at the Department of Media Studies at the University of Education at Winneba from 2007 to 2008.

After his retirement from the Ghana Broadcasting Corporation late 1979, David was appointed United Nations Broadcast Consultant, project coordinator and broadcast expert in 1980. As broadcast expert for the United Nations Educational and Scientific and Cultural Organization (UNESCO), David worked at the UNESCO head offices in Paris. Subsequently, he served in nine African countries: Botswana, Kenya, Lesotho, Namibia, Swaziland, Tanzania, Zambia, Zanzibar and Zimbabwe, where he advised them on setting up and running broadcast network systems. In Zambia, where he spent a considerable amount of time, he trained 40 pioneer broadcasters to run that country's broadcasting system.

In 1984, David was invited by Flight Lt. Jerry John Rawlings, then Chairman of the Provisional National Defense Council (PNDC), to return to the Ghana Broadcasting Corporation as director of Television Unit. David was promoted to deputy director-general and ultimately acting director-general of the entire corporation. His second stint with GBC lasted five years. Two major celebrations were held during his tenure as director-general: the Golden Jubilee of the Corporation in 1985, and "Television comes of Age at 21 in 1986". Guest speakers for the two occasions were Professor P. A. V. Ansah, then Director of the School of Communication Studies at the University of Ghana, Legon, and Professor K. B. Dickson, then Vice-Chancellor of the University of Cape Coast. David was also an external examiner for the Ghana Institute of Journalism in broadcast journalism from 1992 through 1994.

Post Retirement Profession

When David retired a second time from the Ghana Broadcasting Corporation in 1989, he decided to continue his broadcasting career and also as a community leader. He set up a radio station, Radio Peace 88.9 MHz FM, as a non-governmental organization (NGO) in Winneba. He was able to do this with financial assistance from UNESCO, Ford Foundation and DANIDA. This was the first ever community radio station in the Central Region, Ghana, if not the entire country. The station made its debut in June 1999.

David's primary goal in setting up the radio station was to use that media to share the news of events happening in the local community, the Central Region and the country at large. His other goal was to educate, promote and instill self-esteem in his listeners. According to the mission statement, the aim is to "push back the frontiers of superstition, ignorance and illiteracy, filth, disease and conflict…It is to give voice to the voiceless and power to the vulnerable". The Ghana Journalists Association and the Effutu Traditional Council have honored David for the important role that the radio station has played towards improving lives in the community.

Achievements and Awards

As part of Ghana's 51st republic day celebrations in October 2011, David was honored with one of the highest and most coveted awards in the country, "The Order of the Volta". The award was presented to him by the then President, Professor John Evans Atta Mills, for his remarkable public service. David was also chairman of the Programs Commission of the Union of Radio and Television

Organizations of Africa (URTNA). He was a member of the boards of several organizations including Ghana Broadcasting Corporation, the National Film and Television Institute (NAFTI), Ghanaian Times, Wesley Grammar School and Ghana Prisons. He was an author and co-author of five books. He was also an external examiner for the West African Examinations Council (WAEC).

Family Life

David was raised a Methodist and held several positions in the church. He started singing at age eleven with the Winneba Ebenezer Methodist Church Choir, and continued through secondary school, college and university. He worshipped at the Mt. Olivet Methodist Church in Dansoman, Accra, where he was a conference member, member of the Accra Synod, a local preacher, a Bible class leader and a member or patron of several organizations in the church. His last project for the church was helping establish a public relations desk at the head offices of the Ghana Methodist Church in Accra. This project was completed in 1995. He loved sacred, classical and gospel music.

At his death on 10th January, 2016, David left behind his wife, Mrs. Jane Ghartey-Tagoe, the former Miss Jane Micah Sam, of 58 years, son Papa Kwesi Wi, an academician and journalist, daughter Nana Adwowa Ehun, an employee benefits consultant, son Nenyi Kodwo Pere, an attorney, and nine grandchildren. He also left behind several nieces and nephews that he and his wife, Jane, raised and called children.

Mrs. Efua Amakyewa Mills-Robertson

Early Years and Education

E fua Amakyewa was born in Winneba on Friday, 1st August, 1930, to Robert James Sam and the former Grace Andam. Efua Amakyewa, as she was known growing up, was the second born and the only girl among seven children. Three of her siblings, K. G. Sam, Sr., Sagoe Sam and Kwesi Abbey Sam are featured elsewhere in this book. Efua started her formal education at the Methodist Primary School in Winneba in 1936. She continued her elementary school education at the Methodist Middle School, Winneba, from 1942 and completed in 1946.

In school, Efua Amakyewa was quite precocious. This gave her considerable advantage over her colleagues in class work. Her talents were celebrated in her final year at the middle school with an exhibition of her 'Home Work' during Parents' Day. Her high scores during the dreaded Monday morning mental arithmetic often brought her into scuffle with the boys who envied her ability to get them all correct. She always ranked among the top three in class examinations. After completing her elementary school education in 1946, Efua got a scholarship that took her to Wesley Girls' High School, Cape Coast, which she completed in 1950. She continued her education at Wesley College, Kumasi, for her Post Secondary Teacher Training in 1951, ending in 1952 with the Professional Certificated A Teacher's certificate.

Career Path

Efua Amakyewa was an educationist throughout her working life. To her, teaching was not just a profession but a vocation and a "calling". Her role and responsibility as an educator spanned three decades. She taught at the Methodist Primary and Girls Middle Schools in Winneba from 1953 through 1965. She was promoted to the head teacher position in 1965, a position she held until 1973, when she was transferred to Accra. In Accra she continued her career as a classroom teacher till she completed and passed her Principal Teacher Program. She then moved into the inspectorate and supervisory ranks in the Accra Education District Office, providing leadership training to staff and teachers in the district. Efua was transferred to Cape Coast in 1979, where she continued her role as Principal Teacher of Schools till she retired in 1983.

Family Life

After retirement from the school system, Efua Amakyewas and her late husband, Mr. Henry Acquah Mills-Robertson, worked at the "Henry and Efua Education Center". The Center was established by their late son, Mr. Charles Cruickshank Mills-Robertson, in their honor. Fortunately, she lived long enough to see the school achieve the vision as a place of academic excellence.

Efua Amakyewa was born into a home where her father was a Methodist Church Catechist, an administrator and a local preacher, and her mother was a Church Leader and a principal member in various groups in the Winneba Ebenezer Methodist Church. Efua therefore started her life as a Christian. She became a chorister at the age of twelve in 1942, and continued to do so till she was in her 70's. She had a strong but smooth alto voice and sang that part in the choir all her life. Efua became a certified local preacher in 1952, and was appointed a leader in the local church in 1954. Her husband, Henry, was instrumental in forming the Ghana Association of Methodist Church Choirs (GHAMECC), where he served as the first national secretary, vice chairman and later chairman of the Association.

Efua Amakyewa was a founding member of the Winneba Methodist Youth Fellowship. She taught in the Sunday School from 1953 to 1960. She was a member of the Methodist Women's Fellowship and held the position of secretary of the Winneba District. She became a member of the Winneba District Synod in 1961, and was a member of the National Conference of the Methodist Church for several years. She was the district representative of the Methodist General Purposes Committee (GPC) from 1992 through 1997.

For many years, Efua Amakyewa held confirmation classes and prepared young Christians for reception into membership of the Methodist Church, a role her father had performed with distinction for several years in the Winneba Ebenezer Methodist Church. In her later years as a Church Leader, Efua was a counselor and a teacher for the youth group in their 20s and 30s. She fellowshipped with them, and 'walked side-by-side' with them through their faith journey. She helped instill in her wards, Christian discipline, discipleship, a sense of duty to self, others and God. Simply put, she taught them how they could be like Christ in their rela-tionships. Most of these young people saw in her, a mother with compassion, patience, kindness, gentleness, honesty and a good listener. She was an inspiration to the youth in the Church.

Efua Amakyewa's contribution to the Methodist Church, Ghana, was recognized and was duly honored in 1995 during the cele-bration of the 40th anniversary of the rebuilding of the Winneba Ebenezer Methodist Church. She died on 31st August, 2020, at age 90. She was survived by two siblings, four children, several nephews, nieces, in-laws, grandchildren and great grandchildren.

Mr. Kweku Sagoe Sam

Early Life and Education

Kweku Sagoe Sam was born in Winneba on 3rd April, 1935. He was the fourth child of Robert James Sam and the former Miss Grace Andam. His three other siblings, K. G. Sam, Sr., Efua Amakyewa Mills-Robertson and Kwesi Abbey Sam are featured elsewhere in this book. "Segu" as his relatives, peers and friends affectionately called him, began his formal education at the Methodist School, Winneba in 1941 and completed in 1950. He was admitted to Mfantsipim Secondary School in 1951 and passed the Cambridge School Certificate in 1955. Segu completed the two-year sixth-form course and passed the Cambridge Higher School Certificate Examination in 1957. He got a job with the Railway and Harbors Authority soon after that. In 1958, Segu was sponsored by the Authority to study for his bachelor's degree in mechanical engineering at the Kwame Nkrumah University of Science and Technology (KNUST) in Kumasi.

Career Path

Segu went to Britain for a two-year practical attachment with the British Railway Authority in 1965. He became a chartered engineer (C. Eng.) and a member of the Institution of Mechanical Engineers (M.I. Mech. E.) in 1969. After working with the Railway and Harbors Authority for more than a decade, Segu was seconded to Cocoa Products Factory as a Workshop Engineer. During this period, he took several managerial courses, and toured several cocoa processing factories in Europe. On return to Ghana in 1978, he was made a Factory Manager at the Cocoa Products Company.

Segu worked with the West Africa Mills as Deputy General Manager in charge of production. In 1983, he again under-took a three-month course in Vehicle Engineering at Leyland in Manchester, England. He returned to Ghana to head the haulage division of Produce Buying Company, COCOBOD, until his retire-ment in 1985.

After retirement, Segu worked for a year with RESIGHA as the Central Regional Area Manager. Resigha was a subsidiary of J. S. Cocoa, a company that exported raw cocoa to the Netherlands. Segu also served as plant manager at Brosam Limited, a roads construction company, until his death on the 7th September, 1994.

Family Life

Kweku Sagoe Sam was survived by his wife, Joana Nelson, nine Children, namely: Kow Kanyi, Aba Kwegyirba, Kow Eduakwa, Kow Amponsah, Adwowa Abbeyley, Kobina Takyi, Adwowa Brenyewa, Araba Amakyewa and Aba Mansah Sam.

Brigadier General Joseph Nunoo-Mensah (Rtd.)

Early Years and Education

Brigadier Nunoo-Mensah was born in Winneba. He admits he is not sure about his actual date of birth. This fact is not surprising since his parents were both engaged in the fishing industry and never had any formal education. Nunoo-Mensah was told by his parents that he was two years old when the great earthquake occurred in 1939, placing 1937 as his birth year. He reports his birthdate as 14th February, 1937.

As a kid, Nunoo-Mensah helped his parents in their fishing business. Along with other kids, he would pull in the fishing nets after the canoes had landed on the beach. His parents did not want him to go to school, but he wanted to. So he cried and bugged his father until he relented. At the time, there were only four elementary schools in the area. These were the Methodist, Catholic, Anglican and A. M. E. Zion schools. All four were full and were not taking any more students. He was lucky that the Presbyterian Church was about to start an elementary school close to where he lived with his parents. So he was enrolled in the school which was housed in a cocoa warehouse operated by Millers Company. He was much older than all the other kids so he was put in primary class two instead of the usual primary class one for beginners. The school started with ten students, eight boys and two girls. Nunoo-Mensah later transferred to the Winneba Methodist Middle Boys School.

Nunoo-Mensah passed the common entrance examination and was admitted to Agona Nsabaa Secondary School. Living and teaching conditions at the school were less than desirable, so he left and went back to the Winneba Methodist Middle Boys School, where he completed standard seven in 1954. He was 20 years old when he was admitted to the Ghana Secondary School also in Winneba. Conditions at the school were no better than those at Agona Nsabaa. So he and four students wrote a letter to the then Prime Minister, Kwame Nkrumah, complaining about conditions in the school. They never expected to hear from the Prime Minister. To the surprise of Joseph and the four friends, a few months later, a white lady, Ms. Gibson, was posted to the school as principal, and conditions began to change for the better. Ms. Gibson became Nunoo-Mensah's benefactor and mentor. She allowed him to sleep in her living room because she found that conditions at Joseph's home were not conducive to learning. She arranged for him to get a government scholarship which enabled him to stay and complete secondary school.

In Nunoo-Mensah's final year at the Ghana Secondary School in Winneba, the school was visited by a group of white senior army officers who spoke to the students about careers in the military. Nunoo-Mensah jumped at the opportunity, with nothing to lose. He passed the entrance examination and was enrolled at the Ghana Military Academy in 1960. After one year, based on their outstanding performance at the academy, he and three cadets were selected to go to the military academy at Sandhurst in England. Sandhurst was the highest and most prestigious military institution in Britain where cadets from all over the Commonwealth went for officer training. He graduated in 1963 as the best foreign cadet. He returned to Ghana in August 1963.

Career in the Military

On his return from Sandhurst, Nunoo-Mensah was sent to Takoradi in August 1963. A year later, he was promoted to colonel and transferred back to Accra where he was posted to Military Intelligence. Economic conditions in the country had begun to deteriorate with the collapse of the price of cocoa on the world market. Shortages of food were rampant and long queues of people had begun to form at major markets to purchase essential food items. Several attempts were made on the life of Kwame Nkrumah and the security situation in the country was quite tense.

Nunoo-Mensah was at Burma Camp on the morning of 24th February, 1966 when he heard that a military coup had taken place, and that Kwame Nkrumah's government had been overthrown. President Kwame Nkrumah had left the country for China a few days earlier on a mission to end the war in Vietnam. The country had never experienced a coup before so there was confusion among the civilian population. Nunoo-Mensah observed that even those in the military who were not involved in the coup, were confused. Nunoo-Mensah called the army commander, General Bawah, who also did not know what was going on.

It was later learned that the coup, codenamed "Operation Cold Chop", had been planned by some senior army officers including Colonel Emmanuel K. Kotoka who was commander of the Second Infantry Brigade, Lt. Colonel Alphonse Kattah, Colonel Albert K. Ocran who was commander of the First Infantry Brigade, Lt. Colonel David C. K. Amenu, Major Victor Coker-Appiah, Major Lawrence Okai, Major Akwasi Amankwaa Afrifa and Captain Francis Kwashie. John W. K. Harlley, Commissioner of Ghana Police and Anthony K. Deku, Commissioner of Criminal Investigation Department, were also part of the coup plotters.

The pretext used by the senior army officers involved in the coup was that the troops were being moved from Kumasi to Accra to prepare them for their mission to Southern Rhodesia, now Zimbabwe. African nationalists in Southern Rhodesia were fighting for their independence from the British at the time, and President Kwame Nkrumah had announced to the military leadership that some of Ghana's battalions would be sent to Southern Rhodesia to help with the struggle for independence. Consequently, there was no suspicion by any of the senior army officers or heads of the security agencies who were not involved in the plot, when they saw those troop movements towards Accra.

After the army officers had consolidated their hold on the country, most senior military officers not involved in the coup, including Nunoo-Mensah's bosses, were arrested and impris-oned. Nunoo-Mensah became the head of Military Intelligence by default. The coup makers formed the National Liberation Council with Lt. General later Brigadier Joseph Arthur Ankrah as chairman. Nunoo-Mensah was posted to the Military Academy at Teshie as commandant and also as instructor. He spent a year in Canada on assignment in 1968.

The government*of the National Liberation Council under General Ankrah lasted from mid-1966 until 30th September, 1969 when Professor Kofi Abrefa Busia, as leader of the Progress Party, won the national elections and became the prime minister. Two major problems faced Busia's administration: high unemployment and a high crime rate. The latter was attributed to the influx of Nigerians who had fled the Biafran war in Nigeria and entered Ghana as refugees. The pressure to resolve those two problems led to the institution of the Aliens Compliance Order on 19th November 1969.

The Aliens Compliance Order forced the deportation of other nationals, mostly Nigerians, who were in the country illegally. Unfortunately, this mass deportation backfired and negatively impacted the economy. This was because many of those deported had been engaged in transportation and marketing of food and other essential items in the country. This led to widespread discontent throughout the country. It was therefore not surprising when Busia's administration was overthrown by General Ignatius Kutu Akyeampong on 13th January, 1972.

General Akyeampong was chairman of the National Liberation Council and became de facto head of state. Living conditions in the country continued to worsen with food shortages, leading to widespread demonstrations by workers and students. These demonstrations led to the resignation of General Akyeampong on 5th July, 1978 as head of state. Lt. General Frederick William Kwasi Akuffo replaced General Akyeampong as head of state under the governing body's new name, the Supreme Military Council.

It is reported that corruption within the senior military ranks became widespread as they took on civilian roles and responsibilities. The corruption undermined morale among the lower ranks and affected discipline within the military. A common practice then was for Akyeampong and his senior military colleagues to award licenses to their women friends to import anything they wanted including basic foodstuffs like rice, flour, sugar, milk etc. These food items were sold to the public at high prices leading again to protests and demonstrations. The extravagant lifestyles of the military elite, while the masses suffered, did not sit well with many junior military officers and the rank and file of the military. Besides, the importation of those items undermined domestic production and manufacturing which seriously affected efforts by the country to be less reliant on imports.

The frustrations among the junior officers and the rank and file soldiers created conditions that led to Jerry J. Rawlings' first coup attempt on 15th May 1979. This coup failed and Rawlings and his fellow coup-plotting officers were arrested. It is reported that at his trial for treason, Rawlings claimed full responsibility for the failed coup attempt, and pleaded with the presiding senior military officers to punish him alone and let the others go. It was this bold stand by Rawlings, who was willing to take the blame for the failed coup, that endeared him to the rank and file in the army. On 4th June, 1979, junior officers were able to stage a second coup that overthrew the Supreme Military Council government. This time the coup was successful. The officers went and released Rawlings from jail and installed him as leader of the Armed Forces Revolutionary Council (AFRC). Within a short three-week period, Rawlings instituted the "house cleaning" in the military. The house cleaning started with the arrest and summary execution of General Akyeampong, and Major-General E. K. Utuka, commander of the Border Guards on 16th June. This was followed by the execution of generals Akuffo, Afrifa, and Robert E. A. Kotei, Air Vice-Marshall George Y. Boakye, Rear Admiral Joy Amedume and Colonel Roger Felli, a few days later.

Senior military officers who were not executed were arrested and detained, and some had their heads shaved and beaten. Some had their ears used as ash trays, pricked with pins and deprived of sleep. Anger at the market women retailers, who were profiting from their relationships with the top military officials, led to the rank and file soldiers raiding and confiscating goods at Makola Market, the city's central and largest market. This market was bombed and demolished on 20th August, 1979. Nunoo-Mensah escaped all of that because when the soldiers went to arrest him at his house, he ran and hid under the roof of his house! When questioned in an interview years later why a high-ranking military officer of his stature ran and hid to avoid capture, he drew the difference between a soldier dying in battle for a worthy cause and surrendering needlessly to be slaughtered by a band of out-of-control rank-and-file soldiers.

Nunoo-Mensah was appointed Chief of Defense Staff after the military coup that ushered in the AFRC in June 1979. In that position he became head of the country's armed forces and was responsible for the administration and operational control and command of the military. He also became a member of the ruling AFRC. The Armed Forces Revolutionary Council, true to its word, held general elections five months after taking over control of the country's administration. The November 1979 general elections brought in the People's National Party (PNP) led by President Hilla Limann.

Relations between the Limann administration and the military become strained given the various coups that Rawlings had engineered. Rawlings and the top military officers, who had worked with him, were forced to retire from the military and were banned from all military installations. This didn't sit well with the military. Nunoo-Mensah recalls how Joseph de Graft Johnson, Limann's vice-president, called him to his office a few months after Limann became president and asked him to resign and retire from the military. Nunoo Mensah was only 42 years old at the time.

Nunoo-Mensah was subsequently appointed managing director of Ghana Industrial Holding Corporation (GIHOC), and put in charge of all the industries and factories established by Kwame Nkrumah to transform the country's economy. After a few years at the helm of GIHOC, Nunoo-Mensah retired and moved to Haatso, a suburb of Accra, where he established a farm.

President Hilla Limann's People's National Party government lasted only nineteen months, when Jerry Rawlings staged another coup on 31st December, 1981. Nunoo-Mensah was brought back into the Provisional National Defense Council (PNDC) government on 2nd January, 1982. However, after only ten months on the Council, Nunoo-Mensah resigned along with the Rev. Vincent Kwabena Damuah. He attributed his resignation to his disagreement with the policies of the PNDC and the direction in which the country was headed under Jerry Rawlings. It was also during this time that four high court judges were abducted and brutally murdered. Nunoo-Mensah fled the country soon after his resignation from the government in 1983 because he feared for his life.

Nunoo-Mensah in Politics

During the 1992 elections, Nunoo-Mensah entered politics when he stood as the parliamentary candidate for the Awutu-Effutu constituency which included Winneba. He lost the election to Mike Hammah who became the minister of transportation in the new government. Nunoo-Mensah spent one year in India before moving to England. In the meantime, Rawlings had transitioned from chairman of the military Provisional National Defense Council to civilian president on 7th January, 1993, as leader of the newly formed National Democratic Congress.

Nunoo-Mensah returned to Ghana in 1996 and joined the New Patriotic Party (NPP) and managed Nana Akuffo-Addo's campaign for the party's presidential nomination in 1998. Akuffo-Addo lost to John Agyekum Kuffuor who became president. Nunoo-Mensah later left NPP and joined the National Democratic Congress (NDC) and was very active in the December 2008 national elections. When the NDC won the elections, Nunoo-Mensah was appointed National Security Advisor to President John Evans Attah Mills. When Attah Mills died on 24 July, 2012, and John Mahama became the new president, Nunoo-Mensah and others who had served as advisors to Mills were all retired. Currently he does not belong to any political party. He calls himself a patriot, with his main goal being to do as much as he can to improve the lives of his fellow citizens.

Philanthropy

Being a military person and a man of action, Nunoo-Mensah has translated his patriotism into action. He has been involved in many community projects. When he learned that O'Rielly Secondary School, a private school in Accra, was in danger of closing due to lack of funding in 2010, he provided funds that enabled the school to relocate from Asylum Down to Teshie where he had a ten-class-room block built for the school. Apart from providing the money for the classroom block, he was physically and directly involved in the construction of the building, working alongside the artisans and providing food for them as well. So far he has built schools in Agona-Nsabaa, his alma mater, and at Dawurampong in the Central Region. He has also had a hospital built at Kwanyako. He will always be remembered for his charitable spirit.

Family Life

Nunoo-Mensah is at peace with himself, enjoying family and friends. He talks to the media quite frequently about matters of national importance and wishes the country's leaders would truly prove themselves as leaders.

*Source of information on administrations since 1957:

Ghana Government: Ghana National Reconciliation Commission Report, October 2004, Vol. 4, Ch. 1. Security Services.

Colonel Kofi Abaka Jackson (Rtd.)

———○◁◈◈◈▷○———

Early Years and Education

C olonel Jackson was born on 24th September, 1937 in Senya Beraku. His father was Mr. Kwesi Du Jackson, a mason by profession, from Senya Beraku and mother was from Winneba. Kwesi Du Jackson was the younger brother of Mr. Daniel Kwesi Abbiw Jackson, the father of Abbiw, Joseph, Osborne and Ebenezer Jackson, all profiled in this book. Colonel Jackson started his elementary education in 1944 in Senya Beraku. His professional career began in 1953 when he was employed as a tally clerk with Elder Dempster Lines, the largest cargo and passenger shipping company in the country then. His work involved recording goods imported into and exported out of the country through the Port of Winneba. As described above regarding the role that the port played in the colonial era, ships would dock about a mile out to sea and the goods would be rowed in and out in boats to the ships anchored far out. That was before the modern harbor was built at Tema close to Accra.

Colonel Jackson went to Ghana Secondary Technical School (GSTS) in Takoradi, graduating in 1959. He was admitted in 1960 to the Tarkwa School of Mining, now University of Mines, where he enrolled in the Mining Engineering Program. He was one of the first students at the school. However, after six months, he left the mining school to join the military, enrolling at the Military Academy in Accra in April 1960. He graduated from the Ghana Flying Training School in 1962. He served in the air force as transport pilot on the Caribou aircraft. He qualified as a flying instructor in 1963 and by 1970, he was a combat pilot.

Career Path

Colonel Jackson held several positions within the Ghana Air Force. He was commander of the Flying Training School, flew No. 4 Jet Squadron and was director of the Air Force stations in Takoradi and Accra. He also served in the country's administration in various capacities. He was minister of Works and Housing from October 1975 to November 1976, minister of Local Government from November 1976 through July 1977, and Military Secretary at the Ministry of Defense from January 1978 through June 1979.

Colonel Jackson was a member of a six-person group of experts from various countries that advised the United Nations Secretary General on global military resources and the environment in February 1991. The other experts came from the Soviet Union, China, Europe, North America and South America. He represented Africa. Colonel Jackson was also part of a United Nations delegation at an international conference on the "Conversion of Military Resources into Civilian Use". He served as managing director of Ghana Airways from July 1991 through January 1993, chairman of the Technical Committee of the Institute of Industrial Research Management Board, chairman of the Union Rural Bank and a member of the Center for Technology-Driven Economic Development (CTED).

The highlight of his career in the Ghana Air Force was when he led 30 planes in a "Big Formation" for a fly past during Ghana's Independence Day parade celebration in 1974.

Political Prisoner

A dark period in the Colonel's life was on 31st December 1981 when Flight Lieutenant Jerry John Rawlings overthrew the civilian administration of Dr. Hilla Limann and installed the Armed Forces Revolutionary Council (AFRC). Colonel Jackson was one of several ministers and senior government officials who were arrested and imprisoned at Nsawam. He was in prison from early 1982 through January 1984. As described in detail elsewhere in this book, this was indeed a dark period for many people, especially anyone who had either served in government at the highest levels or had been a public figure. He wrote his first book "When Gun Rules" while he was in prison.

Achievements and Awards

Colonel Jackson had an inventive mind and consequently had a number of inventions. He patented three of these inventions. He had his first invention when he was a high school student at Ghana Secondary Technical School in Takoradi. That invention was a perpetual motion machine using eleven magnet bars. The three items he has patented are: Diabetic Therapy which is meant to help control blood-sugar level in humans, Flapping Turbine, and a Compressor/Turbine Rotor. The rotor enhances the performance of turbo engines and machines. He also designed the Cold Running Turbo Charger and Veregreco Solar Dryer. The solar dryer is a vertically ventilated greenhouse solar-powered system. He invented Marine Propeller, Helicopter Rotor and also an Aero Propeller. Another invention is the Float Battery-Charging System which can be used to charge batteries of electric vehicles and aircraft while they are in motion or flight. He also invented a VacVap Fuel System.

Colonel Jackson had several awards in his lifetime. His first award was the Sword of Honor which he got as the best student pilot in February 1962. He was awarded the Special Recognition Award while he was with the Ministry of Environment, Science and Technology. He got the Gold Award for Technology and Research from the African Industrial Pinnacle Award in 2004. He was awarded the Companion of the Order of the Volta in 2007. He won first prize at the 50th anniversary celebration competition in December 2009 from the Council for Scientific and Industrial Research (CSIR). He also won the Millenium Excellence Award in December 2010. His final award was conferred on him at the first Ghana Science Congress in 2011.

Colonel Jackson died on Saturday, 8th November 2021. He was survived by his children, several grandchildren, cousins, nephews and nieces.

Mr. Kwesi Abbey Sam

Early Years and Education

Kwesi Abbey Sam was born in Winneba on 21st January, 1940, the seventh child to Mr. Robert James Sam (Kofi Kanyi) and the former Grace Andam (Ekuwa Kwegyirba). His older brothers K. G. Sam Sr., and Sagoe Sam and older sister Efua Amakyewa Mills-Robertson are featured in this book.

Abbey Sam, as he is called, started his primary education in 1946 at the Winneba Methodist School. He lived with his sister, Efua Amakyewa Sam, at Egyaa-Nomabo Fie in 1953 when his father was serving as catechist and local preacher at Bawjiase. In 1954, when he was in Standard Six or Middle Form 3, he lived with his older brother, K. G. Sam, at Annie Blank House in Winneba.

Older brother, K. G. Sam, had just come out of Wesley College and was assigned to Standard 6A at the Winneba Methodist School. K. G. taught him both at home and school. Kwesi successfully passed the Common Entrance Examinations in 1954 and entered Mfantsipim Secondary School the following year.

Abbey Sam lived in Lockhart House during his seven years secondary education at Mfantsipim. He passed the High School Ordinary Level examination in December 1959, and the Advanced Level examinations in December 1961. Mr. Francis Lodowick Bartels was his headmaster, most of that time, with Rev. W. G. M. Brandful finishing during his last year.

After Mfantsipim, Abbey Sam was admitted to the Kwame Nkrumah University of Science and Technology in Kumasi to pursue a course in civil engineering. He graduated with a bachelor's degree in June 1965. He worked for three years with the Ghana National Construction Corporation (GNCC) as an assistant engineer before proceeding to the Champaign-Urbana campus of the University of Illinois to pursue his master's degree in civil engineering, with specialization in highways and road transportation engineering. He participated in an International Training course in Western Australia September-November 1973, and in the Preparation, Evaluation and Management of Highway Projects – E.D.I., with the World Bank in Washington DC from October to December 1977. In addition, Kwesi has participated in several international workshops from 1976 to 2002.

Career Path

Abbey Sam started work in June 1965 as an Assistant Engineer at the Materials Laboratory of the Ghana National Construction Corporation (GNCC) at Weija, near Accra. In 1966, he was posted to the Survey and Design Division. After the 24th February, 1966 coup that overthrew Kwame Nkrumah's government, GNCC was split into two units, namely the Public Works Department and the State Construction Company. He remained at the Survey and Design Division, then under the Public Works Department. In 1967, he was included in the team for the study, design and construction of a major highway linking Accra and Kumasi, Kumasi and Takoradi and Takoradi to Accra. Accra, Kumasi and Takoradi were the major cities that formed the bedrock of the country's economy. This project was later discontinued by Busia's Progress Party administration when it came into power in October 1969. The new government, dubbing it "The Golden Triangle", did not believe that the project was necessary for the country's economic growth. Abbey Sam left the country to pursue his master's degree which he completed in October 1970.

Abbey Sam returned to Ghana after his master's degree and was posted to Takoradi in October 1970 as the District Engineer for the Public Works Department. While at this post, he helped design and supervised the construction of roads, bridges and other civil engineering projects in several districts in the Western Region. Abbey Sam went to Western Australia for a three-month attachment program with the Main Roads Department of Australia, during this time.

Towards the end of 1973, Abbey Sam was posted to the head office to serve under Mr. H. D. Pappoe in the Roads Planning Division of the Public Works Department. In 1974, he was assigned to the secretariat that planned and executed the change-over from driving on the left to right side of the road throughout the country. The change-over was popularly as "Operation Keep Right". Abbey Sam, as the lead engineer, coordinated all the events that went into the program for the successful change-over in August 1974.

The Ghana Highway Authority was established soon after the implementation of the change-over operation. In 1975, Abbey Sam was appointed as the first Chief Engineer for Road Maintenance. From this position, he rose to deputy chief executive serving in

Administration and Maintenance, then Acting Chief Executive in 1992. In the meantime, the government developed a modern Maintenance Management System for roads in Ghana. Abbey Sam oversaw the installation of the system in the Districts, trained the staff and monitored the implementation. The system became so popular that the World Bank, which had funded the program, decided to implement it throughout the developing world.

In September 1993, Abbey Sam was appointed the chief director of the Ministry of Roads and Highways under the new National Democratic Party (NDC) civilian administration. In 1997, the Roads and Highways Ministry was combined with the Ministry of Transport into a single Ministry of Roads and Transport. Abbey Sam remained the chief director till his retirement in December 2000.

Post Retirement

Since his retirement, Abbey Sam has been involved in several projects as a consultant on his own or with other consulting firms. The following are some of the projects and positions he has held: From 2001 to 2004, Abbey Sam served as an advisor to the Ministry of Roads and Highways on the Implementation Plan and Implementation of the Road Sector Development Program (RSDP). This program was financed by the World Bank. He worked with a Team of Experts on the Evaluation of the Management and Financing Arrangement for Road Maintenance in Ghana, known as the Ghana Road Fund. This was financed by DANIDA, a Danish government development agency.

Abbey Sam also implemented strategies for credit and leasing of equipment from plant pools for road construction contractors. This was done under the auspices of the Association of Road Contractors. Prior to that program, each contractor had to purchase every equipment needed for his/her construction projects. Purchasing every piece of construction equipment can be expensive, given that not all equipment is used all the time and at the same time on any one project. Renting or leasing the equipment, as and when needed, was going to provide more flexibility and cost savings. This study was financed by GTZ, a German grant organization.

Between 2004 and 2015, Abbey Sam participated in the following projects and assignments: the Technical Audit of the Ministry of Roads and Transport, participated with a team of experts to develop the National Transport Policy for the Ministry of Transport, taught construction management to members of the Association of Road Contractors with financial assistance from the German government, and participated in the preparation of the Transport Sector Development Program for Ghana. He also led a team to provide Project Management Support for the Transportation and Agriculture Infrastructure Project Activities for the Millennium Development Authority (MiDA), and worked with a consulting group for the development of the National Road Safety Policy from 2008 through 2015.

Between 2015 and 2019, Abbey Sam worked with Vision Consult on three projects: the Public Expenditure and Institutional Review of the Transport Sector for the Ministry of Transport, the Review of the National Transport Policy, and the Expansion of the Railway Line from Kumasi to Paga in the Northern Region. Abbey Sam is currently working with Vision Consult on the Transaction Advisory Services for the Development of the Ghana-Burkina Railway Interconnectivity Project for the Ministry of Railways Development.

Abbey Sam has served on several Boards. Prominent among them are the following: The Ghana Civil Aviation Authority, Public Procurement Authority where he was the first chairman of the Board from August 2004 until February 2009, and the Engineering Council where he is currently Board Chairman. During his professional career, Abbey Sam attended several seminars and workshops and presented papers at some of them.

Family Life

Abbey Sam was born literally into the Methodist Church, with both parents actively involved in the life of the Methodist Church. He regularly attended worship services as a child with his parents and siblings. At Mfantsipim, attendance was compulsory for all students for a fifteen -minute daily worship service before classes. Worship services on Sunday was also compulsory. While at Takoradi, he joined the Bethel Methodist Church, where he was appointed a leader in 1971. As leader, as his father did at the Winneba Methodist Church, Abbey Sam taught Mfantse to members of the church who had no formal education.

When Abbey Sam finally moved to Accra, he joined the Calvary Methodist Church. Here again, he continued teaching Mfantse. He was a lay leader and organized youth services. He led the Accra Airport Area Bible Class. He was one of the founders of the Immanuel Society now located at the Regimanuel Gray Estate at East Airport in Accra. He is responsible for the orientation classes for persons who want to join the Society. He is a lay preacher and a teacher at the Lay Preachers School.

Mr. Joseph Ebow Bannerman

Early Years and Education

J oseph was born in Winneba on 13th August, 1940. He was the fourth of six children. His parents were Joseph Bannerman and Alice Aryee both from Winneba. Joseph started his education at the Winneba Methodist Primary and Middle Schools and continued to Accra Academy with a full scholarship from the United Africa Company. The United Africa Company ran a scholarship program for children of its employees, and Joseph's father, Jacob, had worked with the company for several years. From Accra Academy Joseph went to Prempeh College in Kumasi for his sixth-form education. He then went to the University of Ghana, Legon in 1962 where he graduated in 1965 with a bachelor's degree in economics. Joseph obtained his master's degree in regional planning from the Kwame Nkrumah University of Science and Technology

(KNUST), Kumasi in 1967. He received a postgraduate diploma in Regional Development Planning from the Settlement Study Centre in Rehovot in Israel in 1971.

Career Path

After graduating from KNUST in 1967, Joseph joined the Ministry of Finance and Economic Planning where he was posted to Cape Coast as the Regional Economic Planning Officer. The government had established economic planning offices in the seven regional capitals. These planning officers were responsible for preparing regional budgets and monitoring government projects in the regions. In 1973, the government decided to use the regional planning offices as agents to transform the economy of the country. Consequently, the government renamed these regional offices, Regional Development Corporations.

The regional development corporations were charged with two major responsibilities. The first responsibility was to assemble baseline data on resources and development opportunities that would be available to private individuals or companies that were looking for areas for investment. The second responsibility was to implement projects that would create jobs and help bring about social and economic development in those regions. Joseph became the first director of the corporation in Cape Coast, the capital city for the Central Region, in 1973. Under his leadership, the Central Regional Development Corporation (CEREDEC), was able to establish several agricultural, industrial and commercial projects in the region. Projects that were established included the Cape Coast Quarry, the Cape Coast Brick and Tile factory, and a wood processing factory at Asin Fosu. Two major projects that continue to operate successfully today, albeit under private ownership, are the Twifo Oil Palm Plantations and the Golden Beach Resorts, now Elmina Motel.

Private Consultancy

Joseph left the Ministry of Finance and Economic Planning to start his own consultancy, Plan Consult, in 1980. His first major project was serving as project economist to the Ministry of Planning in Seychelles through the Commonwealth Secretariat from 1982 through 1983. He has undertaken several projects since then. The following are the projects Joseph has undertaken over the years. Between 1985 and 1987, he did a study on Maize Storage for the Ghana Grain Warehousing Company, undertook a field mission to Lusaka, Zambia, for a Food and Agricultural Organization (FAO) project, and participated in a seminar on Performance Evaluation and Strategic Planning for the African Development Bank (ADB) Training center in Abidjan, Cote d'Ivoire. He also did feasibility studies on Foundation Food Centers for Rokupr in Sierra Leone, Zaria in Nigeria, Marabadicissa in Cote d'Ivoire and Molodo in Mali on behalf of the Economic Community of West African States (ECOWAS) Executive Secretariat in Lagos.

Joseph did three feasibility and evaluation studies during 1990 and 1991: the first was a mango project for UKAYS, a private Ghanaian company, the second was on National Development Planning Capabilities in Ghana under a United Nations Development Program project, and the third on Irrigation-Based Vegetable and Rice Project at Weija for the Ghana irrigation Development Authority in collaboration with the European Union.

Joseph worked on four projects between 1991 and 1993: the Restructuring and Reclassification of Fourteen State-Owned Enterprises and Organizations in Ghana, for the Ghana State Enterprises Commission, Spatial Variations of Social and Economic Facilities in Ghana for the Ghana National Development Planning Commission, Evaluation of Dawhenya Smallholder Rice Irrigation Project for the Ghana Irrigation Development Authority in collaboration with the Ministry Of Food and Agriculture and the European

Union, and the Greater Accra Structure Plan on Employment and Economic Characteristics for the Habitat for Humanity in conjunction with the United Nations Development Program (UNDP).

In 1995, Joseph worked on four projects: a Study on Income-Generating Activities in the Universities for the Ministry of Education in Ghana, a Review of Bilateral Donor-Supported Agricultural Research Projects in Ghana for the Center for Scientific and Industrial Research (CSIR) in Ghana, the Formulation of a Business Development Plan for the Food Research Institute in Ghana, and Market Lot Projects for Adukrom, Apirede and Okrakwodwo in the Akwapim North District, Akyem Akroso and Akyem Akenkanso markets in the Birim South District.

Joseph did an Evaluation of Loan Beneficiaries for the Ministry of Trade and Industries, and the Water Sector Restructuring Project for the Department for International Development from 1997 though 1999. Between 2001 and 2003, he worked on four projects: Preparation of Business Plan for the Ministry of Justice and Attorney General, Development of Human Resource Management System for the National Institutional Renewal Program, Preparation of Business Plan for Ghana Standards Board and Assessment of the Agricultural Sector, and Natural Resource Management Issues in Ghana for the United States Agency for International Development (USAID).

Joseph worked on seven projects between 2004 and 2009. These are Mid-Term Review of the Small-Scale Irrigation Development Projects for the Ghana Irrigation Development Authority, Diagnostic Study of the Public-Private Partnership Projects for the Ministry of Private Sector Development, and the Development of a Business Plan for the Ghana Railway Company for the Ministry of Harbors and Railways. Other studies were the Feasibility Study on the Interconnectivity of the Railway Systems of ECOWAS Member States for the ECOWAS Commission, Ghana Professional Services Export Strategy for the Ghana Export

Promotion Council, Feasibility study for the Ghana Ports of Tema and Takoradi Master Plans for the Ghana Ports and Harbors Authority, and Mid-Term Review of Trade Sector Support Program for the Ministry of Trade and Industry.

Joseph was project manager for six projects in 2010: Feasibility Study and Development of a Business Plan and Investment Strategy and Promotion for the Proposed Hi-Tech Park for the Ministry of Communication, Design and Development of a Training and Development Policy and Strategy Within the Public Service in The Gambia, and Functional and Organizational Assessment of Metropolitan, Municipal and District Assemblies for the Ministry of Local Government and Rural Development. Others were Consultancy Services for the Evaluation of the Ghana Program for Diakonia, Mid-Term Review of the Program for the Promotion of Perennial Crops (oil palm and rubber) in Ghana, for the Ministry of Food and Agriculture, and Assessment of Gender Awareness in Selected Courses at Kofi Annan International Peace Keeping Center.

Between 2011 and 2015 Joseph handled another seven projects: Retooling and Modernizing Ghana Ministry of Tourism into an Effective and Proactive Agency for the Ministry of Tourism, Reactivation of Kpong Farms Limited into a Self-Sustaining Commercial Entity for the Volta River Authority, and Gender Assessment for the Water and Sanitation Sector in Ghana for the Ministry of Water Resources, Works and Housing. The following are the other four projects that were developed during that period: Pre-Feasibility Study for the Accra Plains Public Private Partnership Project, the Development of a Comprehensive Assessment of the Capacity Needs of Land Sector Agencies in Ghana, the Design of Human Resource Development Plans and the Development of Strategic Capacity Building Framework for Ghana's Local Government Service.

Over the years Joseph has served as guest lecturer in project planning at Ghana Institute of Management and Public

Administration (GIMPA), and at the Pan African Institute for Development in Buea in the Republic of the Cameroons. He was also a consultant at a Public Enterprises Seminar at the African Development Bank's Training Centre in Cote d'Ivoire. He was an external examiner for the Master of Science Regional Planning Program at the Kwame Nkrumah University of Science and Technology in Kumasi between 1981 and 1984.

Joseph is currently a board member of the Brussels-based International Consulting Alliance (ICA), a network of organizations and experts, working on development partner-funded coopera- tion projects with the aim of building together a community of trusted partners. Joseph is a past president of Ghana Association of Consultants, past president and Fellow of Ghana Institute of Planners and Fellow of the International Center for Research and Training in Project Management, Montreal, Quebec, Canada.

Awards

He was awarded a D. Litt. (Honoris Causa) degree by the University of Education, Winneba in 2007 for "his immense con- tribution to education and to the social well-being of the people of this country, Africa and the world in general". In May 2021, the University of Education, Winneba, honored him again by naming a lecture theater at the university after him.

Family Life

Joseph is a Christian. He started his faith journey in high school as a member of the Scripture Union often attending youth camps. He has been a long-standing member of the Winneba Ebenezer Methodist Church. He is a dedicated Rotarian and has participated in many community-service projects.

Joseph is married to Valentina and is a father and grandfather. He is a patron to many nephews and nieces. His hobbies are listening to Christian and classical music, tennis, and golf.

Mrs. Felicity Efua Arkhurst

Early Years and Education

Felicity was born on 4th April, 1941 at Nsawam in the Eastern Region and was named Efua Mensima. The oldest of eight children. Her father was Gilbert Samuel Kwesi Mensah, Jnr., and known by family and friends as GSK. Gilbert was the head (ebusua panyin) of Anona clan in Winneba. He worked as a regional officer for the Cocoa Marketing Board for several years, and worked in Dunkwa-on-Offin, Koforidua, Nsawam, Swedru and Nkawkaw before retiring. Efua's mother, Beatrice Odoomah Benyiwa Mensah, als from Winneba, was a baker by profession.

Efua started her primary education at Nsawam Methodist School and continued to Wesley Grammar School in Accra completing in 1962. She trained as a nurse at Korle-Bu Teaching

Hospital in Accra, qualifying as a registered nurse in 1966. She went to London to continue her training at the Charing Cross Hospital and obtained her state midwifery certificate in 1969. She completed her training in 1970 as an intensive care specialist at the same hospital.

Career Path

After qualifying as a registered nurse and midwife, Efua's first job was as a nursing sister at the Intensive Care Unit in Central Middlesex Hospital, Acton, London in 1971. She practiced midwifery for a few years and then moved back into general nursing in 1978. She worked at the Health Centre in Holloway Prisons in London, the biggest female prison, for three years. In 1992, she travelled to Saudi Arabia to work as the third in command to the director of nursing and the deputy at a military hospital in Wadi--Al-Dawasar. She worked briefly at the military hospital in Alfa-Al-Batin, also in Saudi Arabia, before returning to Britain in August 1997. Back in Britain, she worked as the deputy head at a nursing home for Roman Catholic nuns in Kensington, London, till her retirement in 2006.

Community Involvement

Efua returned to Winneba with her husband, Mr. Tom Arkhurst, in 2006. The two decided to set up the Arkcity-Link-Foundation. This foundation was a non-profit educational institution that offered practical training in Information and Communication Technology (ICT) to young people between the ages 6 to 16, mostly persons in primary and junior high schools. Efua and Tom Arkhurst found that many of the schools in Winneba were teaching ICT as a subject but they lacked the basic practical computer practical skills that would complement the students' theoretical knowledge.

The Foundation arranged with the schools to send their students there for two- to three-week training sessions. The Foundation also organized six quiz competitions during the year for all primary and junior high schools in the Winneba Traditional Area. In addition to providing classes in computers, the Foundation held classes that were aimed at empowering the youth with social and other skills that would help them achieve their potential.

While in London, Efua participated in fundraising activities by joining "Coffee Mornings" which raised money for the MacMillan Cancer Research to support the 153,000 people who needed help while in cancer treatment then.

Efua's efforts to provide educational opportunities to the youth in Winneba and support for cancer patients in London were recognized by Ohio University in the United States with an honorary doctorate for outstanding public service in 2017.

Family

Efua has been a member of the Central Hall Methodist Church in Westminster, London for over 15 years and was a church steward working at the welcoming desk. She has also been a member and leader at the Ebenezer Methodist Church in Winneba. She is the chairperson of the Scholarship Committee and also a patron for other Societies including the Church Choir and the Singing Band. She is also a member of the Susanna Wesley Auxiliary Society (Zuma) in London. She has been a mentor to many others in the community.

Efua is married to Tom Arkhurst, a retired accountant in London. Tom has been the brain behind Arkcity-Link- Foundation. They have several children, nephews, nieces and grandchildren.

Rt. Rev. Dr. Joseph Kow Ghunney

Early Years and Education

The Right Reverend Dr. Joseph Kow Ghunney was born in Winneba in 1950. His parents were Kwame Baah Ghansah Ghunney and Ekua Baduwa. He was brought up by his step-father, Kweku Sofo Enninful, his uncle Jonathan Kofi Ackom Ghunney and grandfather Albert Babington Ghunney, the first Ghanaian post-master. Joseph had his elementary school education in Winneba and Cape Coast. After completing middle school, he went to stay with his uncle in Monrovia, Liberia, where he worked as an auto mechanic and a carpenter. He returned to Ghana in 1969 and worked briefly with the Public Works Department in Winneba. He studied on his own and passed the examinations which enabled him to enroll in Abetifi Teacher Training College in 1970.

Career Path

After graduating from Abetifi Training College in 1972, Joseph taught at schools in Kwanyako and Winneba. Three years into teaching, he passed the Ordinary and Advanced level examinations. He then decided to go into the Christian ministry. He enrolled in Trinity College, now Trinity Theological Seminary, near Legon. After completing his studies and earning high marks in his final examinations, he was recruited to teach pastoral studies at the seminary. He was commissioned as a reverend minister in the Methodist Church in 1978 and posted to Kumasi Wesley Church where he served from 1978 through 1981. He was assigned as a missionary to the United Methodist Church in Liberia in 1982. When he returned to Ghana, Joseph was posted to Freeman College in Kumasi as principal of the college. He was also made the superintendent minister for the Kwadaso District also in Kumasi.

Joseph earned his master's degree from the Wesley Theological Seminary in Washington D.C. in 1987. He obtained his Ph.D. in pastoral counseling from Loyola College in Baltimore in 1994. He served many churches while pursuing his graduate studies. His specialties were substance abuse, addictions and peer counseling.

Joseph was a consultant in substance abuse for the United Methodist Church and a coordinator of Shalom Communities in Ghana for the Board of Global Ministries, U.S.A. On returning to Ghana in 1995, Joseph taught at Trinity Theological Seminary. He was later promoted to vice-principal and then dean of students at the seminary. He was also Candidates' Secretary of the Methodist Church, Ghana. Joseph was an adjunct lecturer in psychology and pastoral counseling at the Methodist University College, Ghana, Korle Bu Nurses Training College and counselor to the Planned

Parenthood Association of Ghana. Joseph pastored Calvary Methodist Church in Adabraka, Immanuel Methodist Church in East Airport, Atomic Hills Estate Methodist Church and Ascension Methodist Church in Haatso, near Accra.

Reverend Ghunney was inducted as the Bishop of the Winneba Diocese of the Methodist Church, Ghana in October 2006. Joseph hosted the Methodist Conference held in Winneba in 2008. This conference is held annually and undertaken at different diocesan major towns. Joseph's tenure as bishop ended after the 2012 Annual Conference. After recovering from a brief period of illness which took him to Korle Bu Hospital and the United States, Joseph returned to teaching at the Trinity Theological Seminary and the Methodist University College.

Life as a Methodist and Achievements

As a young boy, Joseph sang in the Winneba Methodist Church Choir, and was a member of the Youth Fellowship. He formed the Winneba Young Peoples Union in the late 1960s and early 70s along with some friends to conduct cleaning operations in the town. While studying for his doctorate in Maryland, Joseph and some friends, notably the Reverends Kofi Bart Martin, John Bonful and John Ansah-Arkoful started ministering to the Ghanaian community as chaplains at social gatherings, including baby out-doorings, birthdays, wedding engagements and ceremonies and funerals. Chatting with friends and discovering that there was a hunger among Ghanaian Methodists in the diaspora for the Ghana Methodist worship service liturgy which included the singing of canticles etc., Joseph and the friends decided to start a church.

The "church" which grew to become the Ebenezer Methodist Church, began with his wife, Cecilia, daughters Yvonne and Aya, Dr. Joseph Atta-Quartey and Dr. Kofi Abruquah. Their first worship service was held in the basement at the home of Dr. Abruquah in Hyattsville in Maryland on 17th May, 1992. The church later moved to College Park with Revd. Ghunney the first minister, Dr. Joe Kofi Atta-Quartey the first organist, and Dr. Kofi Abruquah the first society steward. They later worshipped at the Free United Methodist Church at Layhill with 21 members. After eight months, the church moved to First United Methodist Church on Belcrest Road in Hyattsville. The church is now the North America Mission, a diocese of the Methodist Church, Ghana.

While a doctoral student in the United States, Joseph was chaplain at St. Elizabeth Hospital in Washington, D.C. As a mental health and substance abuse counselor, Joseph worked at the Center for Addiction and Pregnancy at the Prince George's County Health Department in Maryland and also at the Awakening Program at the Prince George's County Department of Corrections, also in Maryland.

During his tenure as bishop, Rev. Ghunney introduced the Ebusua Tow (Family Dues) which raised funds for development projects in Winneba and beyond. He was involved in the Rafiki Orphanage Village at Gyahadze as patron. A description of this project is detailed under Professor John Humphrey Amuasi's profile above. In 2014, Joseph inaugurated the Charis Life Enrichment Center at the Winneba Roundabout. The goal was to train professionals in counseling, pastoral, spiritual care and leadership to serve their families, schools, churches and the society at large. Charis would also serve as a place where people could receive counseling to help with various addictions.

Family Life

The last church Rev. Ghunney pastored was the Ascension Methodist Church in Accra. He died on 13th September, 2016 at Doctors Community Hospital in Lanham, Maryland, after a year's illness. He was survived by his wife, Cecilia, daughters Yvonne and Aya and two grandchildren, Joshua and Gabrielle.

Section D

The Next Generation

Mr. Harvey Joseph Kwesi Gyansa Essilfie

Early Years and Education

Harvey Essilfie was born at Nkawkaw in the Eastern Region on 28th January, 1961. He was the fifth child of his parents, Mr. Rexford Essilfie and the former Ms. Isabella Okorba Amuasi, both from Winneba. His parents settled at Agona Swedru where his father owned a business as a retailer. Harvey attended the Agona Swedru Methodist Primary School in 1965. He continued at the Akropong Presbyterian Boarding School in 1971 for two years and then to Ghana Secondary Technical School in Takoradi in 1973. Harvey got his Ordinary Level certificate in 1977. He continued to the Winneba Secondary School from 1977 through 1979 for his Advanced level certificate. He then attended Kwame Nkrumah University of Science and Technology (KNUST) in Kumasi in 1979, and graduated with a bachelor's degree in engineering mathematics in 1983.

Career Path

Harvey taught mathematics at Swedru Secondary School and then at his alma mater, Takoradi Ghana Secondary Technical School which was renamed Takoradi Polytechnic. He left for Monrovia, Liberia in 1990 where he taught at the B. W. Episcopal School. A few months later into his stay, he was caught up in the Liberian Civil War which forced him to return to Ghana. When he returned to Ghana that year, Harvey taught at the St. Paul Methodist Secondary School at Tema. At his passing in 2003, he was working in the production unit at Aluworks, an aluminum products company, in Tema.

Harvey as a Musician

Harvey developed an interest in music at an early age. At the tender age of eight, he started playing the piano and joined the Agona Swedru Emmanuel Methodist Church choir. Harvey's was a musical family. His mother, Isabella, was a soloist with the Winneba Ebenezer Methodist Church choir in middle school. Harvey's older brother, Rexford Essilfie, Jnr. and his younger brother, Mensah Essilfie, also played the piano, growing up. Recognizing his children's interest in music at those early ages, their father hired Dr. David Egyapong, a professional musician, to teach the boys the rudiments of music. His uncle, Dr. George Amuasi, then in secondary school, helped him with his piano skills whenever he visited the family during the holidays. While in boarding school at Akropong, the headmaster was so fascinated by Harvey's skills that he allowed Harvey to come to his house to play his organ.

During his student years at KNUST, Harvey was a member of the University non-denominational Protestant Chaplaincy choir.

Harvey was appointed organist at the Bethel Methodist Church in Takoradi in 1989, and became the music director for the Greater Takoradi District in the Western Region in 1990. Harvey settled in Tema where he was made the choir director at St. Paul Methodist Cathedral. He was associated with the Hillary Voices, a choir founded by his older brother, Dr. Rexford Essilfie. He was also a member of the Ghana Methodist Students Union, the Full Gospel Business Men's Fellowship, and the Cocoa Processing Company Choir in Winneba.

Harvey composed several types of church music. They ranged from hymns, and anthems to tunes that had the African hi-life rhythm. The latter was a favorite during worship services when members of the congregation would dance to their hearts content during fund-raisers. He was very proficient at the church organ and played the full bass pedal board. His organ playing skills were greatly admired by all those who were privileged to watch him play during and after church services.

Family Life

Harvey was a philanthropist. He devoted his remuneration from the church to helping needy students and also those who were experiencing financial difficulties. He died suddenly on 10th July 2003 when he was only 42 years old. He was survived by his wife, the former Genevieve Naa Tiokor Odonkor, of only four years, and their three children, Rex, Isabella and Harvey Jnr. He left behind three sisters and two brothers.

Professor Ruby Hanson

Early Years and Education:

Ruby was born on 12th April, 1961, the second of six children, and the first of four girls. Her parents were Alfred Isaac Krampa from Agona Asafo and Effuah Eyimbil Krampa, from Winneba. She had her primary school education at the State Experimental School at Nhyiaeso in Kumasi. She attended St. Louis Secondary School also in Kumasi from 1973 through 1980, earning her General Certificate of Education, Ordinary and Advanced Level certificates, in science. Ruby was house prefect while at St. Louis Secondary School. After secondary school she went to Wesley College in Kumasi from 1982 – 1985, where she obtained the post-secondary "Certificate A" with distinction in science and education. She was women's prefect while at Wesley College.

Ruby continued to the University of Education in Winneba in 1988. Ruby was wing commander for Aggrey Hall Block B while a student at the university. She obtained her diploma in chemistry and integrated science, passing with second class upper division in 1991. She went on to do her bachelor's degree program in chemistry and integrated science which she passed with first-class honors in 1997. Ruby entered the University of Cape Coast in 1999 and graduated in 2003 with her M.Phil. degree in chemistry. Ruby did a two-year program, 2006 and 2008, on "Development and Research in Science and Mathematics Education" at the Vrije University in Amsterdam. She started her doctorate program at the University of Education in Winneba in 2010 and earned a Ph.D. in chemistry education in 2014. She did further studies in designing and facilitating E-Learning, Level 5, at the Open Polytechnic of New Zealand from 2014 through 2015.

Career Path

After graduating from Wesley College, Ruby taught at the Advanced Teacher Training College Primary School in Winneba from 1985 through 1987. When the family moved to Akwatia, she taught at the Amanfrom Junior High School from 1987 to 1988. After obtaining her diploma in chemistry and integrated science from the University of Education in Winneba in 1991, Ruby taught at the Akwatia Technical Institute from 1991 to 1994. She took a break in 1994 to work on her bachelor's degree after which she went back to Akwatia to teach at St. Rose's Secondary School from 1997 – 1998.

Ruby joined the teaching staff at the Department of Science Education at the University of Education in Winneba as teaching assistant in 1999. She also served as demonstrator for the Department of Chemistry at the University of Cape Coast in 2003. Ruby became a lecturer at the Department of Science Education at the university in Winneba in 2004. The department's name was changed in 2012 to the Department of Integrated Science

Education. She was promoted to senior lecturer in 2012, vice dean and associate professor in 2016, then dean of the Faculty of Science Education in 2018. Ruby became acting pro-vice chancellor in 2019.

Professional Achievements

Ruby has written five books, contributed chapters in four books, and published approximately 70 articles, individually and with colleagues, in refereed journals. Additionally, she has participated in 50 conferences locally and abroad where she presented papers. She has participated in several seminars and workshops. She has supervised over 180 undergraduate student projects, and thirty-three M. Phil. students. She has been an external examiner for the West African Examinations Council, for students working on their M. Ed., M. Phil and Ph.D. degrees in science education at the University of Pretoria, South Africa, University of Witwatersrand, Johannesburg in South Africa, and the North-Western University in South Africa. She has also been a reviewer for the Journal of Educational Research and Reviews, the African Journal of Research in Mathematics and Science Education, and Science Education International.

Ruby is a member of the Ghana Chemical Society, Ghana Science Association, American Chemical Society, Graduate Women International, Ghana Association of Science Teachers, University Teachers' Association of Ghana, Organization for Women in Science for the Developing World, and Ghana National Association of Teachers. She is an interim executive member of the International Network of Women in Engineering and Science, the African Regional Network. She is a patron of two organizations, the Ghana Chemical Society at the University of Education, Winneba students' branch) and the Association of Science Education Students. She was a member of a joint Ghana-Netherlands Project

(PRACTICAL) on enhancing teaching and learning of science and mathematics from 2006 through 2010, and also a member of the Project Planning Committee, a Ghanaian-Finish Higher Education project in 2016.

Ruby has been instrumental in the following pedagogical innovations at the University of Education, Winneba; Computer-based (hybrid online) Teaching, Micro Science Teaching and the Development of Tiered Diagnostic Assessments for Unearthing Misconceptions. She has served on several professional commit-tees including the following: chairperson for the 26th Congregation Awards Committee, Investigative Committee of Examination Malpractice at Ajumako Campus, Estate Management Committee, University of Education Affiliated-Institutions Monitoring Team (Southern Sector Institutions), Department of Chemistry Education Science Board, and Sexual harassment Committee. She was lead coordinator of American Science Society Chemistry Fair for 2020, 2021 and 2022.

Ruby was a member of the following university committees; Learning Management System Monitoring and Evaluation, the Committee for Launching 2019-2023 Strategic Plan, Committee on Publication of History of the University of Education, Winneba, Awards Selections Committee for Indigenous Students, Committee on Rationalization of School of Creative Arts & Faculty of Home Economics Education Textile and Clothing Course, and the Review of Junior Staff Promotion Criteria and Plagiarism Committee. She has sat on the following boards: University Executive Academic Board, Faculty of Science Education Academic Board, Department of Integrated Science Academic Board, Faculty of Science Education Journal, Departmental Graduate Board for Thesis Supervision, and lastly the Library, Bookshop and Educational Resources Board.

Ruby has been facilitator, moderator or lead discussant for several workshops, seminars and exhibitions. She has served as a mentor for several organizations including female teachers, and trainees for integrating gender into curriculum and for science education.

Awards

Ruby has been the recipient of several certificates and awards from numerous organizations. She received her first awards in 1998 as the Best 3rd Teacher Award in the Kwaebibirem District in Kade in the Eastern Region, Ghana, and a conference participant certificate from the Ghana Association of Science Teachers also in 1998. Since then she has received the following excellence awards: Institute for Educational Development and Extension (2013), International Science Education Conference (2014), University of California at Riverside (2015), and International Conference on Education Research for Development in Africa (2016).

Other awards that Ruby has received have been the International Teacher Education Conference (four times in 2017), South Africa Chemical Institute (2018), International Network of Women Engineers and Scientists (2019), Gordon Research Conference/Chemistry Education, Research and Practice (2019), Canada International Conference on Education (2018 & 2019), and the International Union of Pure and Applied Chemistry/International Conference on Chemistry Education (2016 & 2019). The Canada International Conference on Education/World Education Conference gave her two awards in 2014 and one in 2021. The Clute Institute honored Ruby in 2019.

Family Life

Ruby's hobbies are gardening, reading and listening to Christian music. Mother of four children. She was widowed in August 2009. Apart from English, Ruby is fluent in Fante, Asante Twi and Effutu.

Dr. Kweku Ghartey Sam, Jnr.

Early Years and Education

Kweku was born on 18th August, 1965. His parents were Mr. Kweku Ghartey Sam, Sr. profiled above under Internationals, and the former Ms. Christina Paintsil, both from Winneba. He attended the Datus Preparatory Primary School in Accra. From there he went to Adisadel College in Cape Coast from 1976 through 1983, passing both the General Certificate of Education, Ordinary and Advanced Level, examinations. Kweku was voted head prefect in his final year in high school in 1981.

Kweku spent one year at the University of Ghana, Legon in 1984, then continued to the University of Ghana Medical School at the Korle Bu Teaching Hospital in Accra, where he graduated as a physician. While in medical school, Kweku earned a scholarship to study biochemistry at the University College, London, earning a bachelor's degree in 1991. He did his housemanship at the Departments of Surgery, Child Health and Radiology at Korle Bu Teaching Hospital from 1991 through 1994. Kweku then went to the University of Connecticut Children's Medical Center, where he did his internship and residency from 1994 through 1997.

Professional Career

Kweku has been a pediatrician at Alliance Medical group in Middlebury, Connecticut since 1998. He is a Fellow of the American Association of Pediatrics (FAAP). He is also Faculty Attending at the University of Connecticut, School of Medicine in Harmington, Connecticut. Between 1999 and 2017, he was school physician at the Forman School in Litchfield in Connecticut. He was chairman of the Pediatrics Department at Waterbury Hospital in Connecticut from 2001 through 2003. He was also a member of the Staff Executive Committee at the Hospital during that period. Kweku has been a member of Prospect Waterbury Local Advisory Board at the Hospital. He has co-authored an article that was published in the British Journal of Nutrition in 1989.

Membership in Associations

Kweku is a fellow of the American Academy of Pediatrics, the American Academy of Pediatrics (Connecticut Chapter), Crossroads Outreach Medical Missions International, Oxford Greens Golf Club, Walnut Hill Community Church, Adisadel Old Boys Association (North America), and Santa 81, Adisadel old Boys Association '81 Year group.

Family Life

Kweku is married to Dr. Akua Amponsa Sam. The couple has three children, Kweku, Aba and Kwesi. His hobbies are golf, gardening and reading.

Epilogue

T he main goal of this book is to inspire anyone, young or old, to greater achievement in life.

The remarkable thing about the individuals profiled in the book is how, from very humble and mostly unsophisticated backgrounds, these sons and daughters of Winneba and Senya Beraku were able to rise to the highest levels in their respective fields of endeavor. Some commanded the world stage. Some held leadership positions in the country. Some competed with the best around the world and won. Some held leading positions in institutions hitherto dominated by non-Africans. These achievements give lie to the notion that some racial groups are intellectually inferior to others.

The common thread for all these success stories was the role that education played in their lives. Education was transformational for them. It gave them the ladder on which they advanced from one stage to the next. The advanced industrialized world has known this basic principle for years and has provided universal primary, middle, and secondary education for their citizens as a right. I hope that this lesson will not be lost on Third World Countries like Ghana, still struggling with illiteracy and poverty.

I hope this book will continue a tradition initiated by Magnus Sampson, who wrote "Gold Coast Men of Affairs" in 1937. Magnus' book was the first ever to document the lives of local people who had contributed to the country's social, political and economic development. Since then, autobiographies and biographies of some individual Ghanaians have been written and published. The strength of the current book is that it brings together the lives of many of these individuals in one volume. Sampson's book high-lighted the lives of persons from the entire country. This current book covers the lives of persons from just two towns, and that is remarkable.

This book is written by a Ghanaian, born and raised in Winneba, about persons born and raised in Winneba and Senya Beraku.

CPSIA information can be obtained
at www.ICGtesting.com
Printed in the USA
LVHW070748100522
718323LV00021B/652

9 781662 847271